Wilderness Survival Guide for Kids

Everything You Need to Know to Survive in the Outdoors | Discover How to Build Cozy Shelter, Start a Fire, Evade Animals, Forage for Food, Find Water, and More!

Andrew Brin

Table of Contents

🔥 Introduction
The Joy of Exploring the Wilderness

Exploring undeveloped areas, particularly when one is a child, may be an experience that is both profoundly energizing and freeing. The untamed outdoors provides a stage for imagination, creativity, and the primitive thrill of being one with nature. In a time where screens and scheduled schedules rule the roost, the outdoors provides a haven for these qualities. A brook suddenly carries the promise of buried gold, a woodland morph into a realm straight out of a fairy tale, and a mountain takes on the appearance of a magnificent castle.

The scent of moist dirt, blossoming flowers, and tall pine trees fills the air, giving it a cleaner and fresher feel. The sound of chirping birds, rustling leaves, and the odd call of a far-off animal fill the silence left by the lack of city sounds. This is not only a breath of fresh air for children; rather, it is an immense, real-world playground where they may climb, run, swim, and discover new things.

In addition, the fields and woodlands provide a wide variety of educational opportunities. They teach children about the delicate balance that exists within natural environments, foster a feeling of reverence for all kinds of life, and expose youngsters to a wide variety of ecosystems. In addition to this, it gives one the feeling of having achieved something. Learning to find your way through trails, recognize animal tracks, or even fish in a stream may bring a sense of accomplishment that is unrivaled by the majority of things available in today's world.

There is also the special camaraderie that develops between friends and family members when they go hiking or camping together in the great outdoors. People get closer to one another via overcoming obstacles and making discoveries together, and the memories that they create throughout their travels endure a lifetime. The wilderness serves as a massive, ever-evolving educational facility that encourages inquisitiveness and recognizes valor.

Why Wilderness Survival Skills are Important

Children may learn vital life values such as problem-solving, ingenuity, and resiliency by participating in wilderness survival activities. Confronting one's fears and prevailing over them is a great way to boost one's self-confidence and get better prepared for dealing with difficulties in other aspects of life. A greater respect for professional rescue services and responsible care of environment may be fostered via the acquisition of these abilities, which can also serve as a stepping stone toward the inculcation of other values such as empathy, responsibility, and community service.

In addition, the development of survival skills fosters attributes of leadership and collaboration within a group. Whether it be working together to construct a makeshift shelter or guiding a group to a source of water, these abilities frequently entail the application of collective effort and the making of group decisions. Therefore, educating children in wilderness survival not only gets them ready for unexpected events, but also gives them skills that are applicable in a wide variety of different situations throughout their lives.

In a nutshell, the satisfaction of adventuring in the great outdoors and the realization of the critical nature of acquiring wilderness survival skills are two sides of the same coin. The first makes the journey worthwhile, and the second guarantees that the adventurers can safely handle any problems that they may meet during the quest. Together, they provide an experience that is well-rounded, interesting, and instructive for children, which is beneficial to children in the short term as well as for a significant portion of their future.

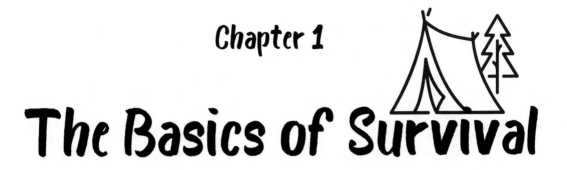

Chapter 1

The Basics of Survival

Understanding the "Rule of Threes"

The "Rule of Threes" is a key idea in wilderness survival that serves as a framework for prioritizing demands under circumstances that pose a significant risk to one's life. This rule places an emphasis on the time restrictions that a person normally has before the loss of various requirements becomes significant. These time limits are as follows: three minutes without air, three hours without shelter in harsh weather, three days without water, and three weeks without food. It is vital for anybody who is going to venture into the wilderness to understand this rule, but it is especially important for children since they may not have the same degree of judgment or experience as adults.

Three minutes with no air in the lungs

It should come as no surprise that air is vitally important, and luckily, the vast majority of the surroundings we encounter outside do not directly endanger our respiratory systems. Nevertheless, this category might include predicaments such as suffocation, drowning, or being hemmed in by walls or other obstacles in an area that has restricted airflow. It is imperative to take prompt action, and having fundamental first aid information such as how to do CPR or the Heimlich maneuver can be a lifesaver. It may make a huge difference in the event of an unexpected crisis if children are taught these fundamental abilities.

Three hours with no protection from the elements

The provision of shelter is of the utmost importance, particularly in situations of severe climate, such as high heat or cold, or heavy rain. A well-constructed shelter can offer protection from conditions such as hypothermia, heatstroke, and dehydration. It is important for children to be taught how to construct impromptu shelters utilizing natural resources such as branches, leaves, and snow, as well as man-made materials such as tarps and space blankets. It is also important to know how to locate a decent location, one that is free from potential dangers such as falling rocks or surging waves.

Three Weeks Without Eating Anything

When it comes to matters of survival, food is far down on the list of priorities. Even though food is necessary for keeping one's strength and morale up, the human body can normally function for a considerable amount of time without it, drawing its energy from the reserves of fat that it has accumulated. If you teach children how to recognize edible plants, construct simple traps, or fish, you can equip them with the skills necessary to locate food in the event that they find themselves in a survival crisis.

When time and resources are limited, the "Rule of Threes" provides an organized strategy to survival, which helps to prioritize activities and determine their order of importance. When there is a crisis, this is a straightforward and efficient method for recalling the information that is most important. By instilling in children, the habit of following this guideline, parents may better their children's capacity for self-reliance and improve their ability to find solutions to difficult problems. It's not only about making sure they stay alive; it's also about establishing in them a feeling of responsibility and awareness that will serve them well throughout their lives, whether they spend it in or out of the wilderness.

The Importance of a Positive Attitude

In the context of surviving in the wilderness, physical components such as water, food, and shelter are frequently emphasized. However, the value of maintaining a healthy mental attitude is sometimes disregarded. Nevertheless, it is an essential component of being able to persevere through difficult circumstances and emerge victorious, particularly for children who may not yet have completely formed coping strategies. A good mental attitude not only boosts your own spirits, but it also has the potential to boost the spirits of people around you, so creating an atmosphere that is mutually encouraging and beneficial to survival.

Psychological toughness or fortitude

Mental toughness may be a critical factor in determining one's success or failure in the face of challenging circumstances. Individuals, particularly youngsters, are able to adjust their behavior to unfavorable conditions if they have a positive attitude, which is directly linked to psychological resilience. When children are taught to have a positive outlook, it makes them more prepared to deal with negative experiences. A cheerful attitude helps clarify the mind, which makes it easier to focus on problem-solving and critical thinking, both of which are vital survival abilities. In summary, a happy attitude makes it easier to survive.

Advantages to One's Body

It might come as a surprise, but one's mental health does have an impact on their physical health. A higher heart rate, faster tiredness, and lowered immunity are all potential outcomes of chronic stress and worry. A more optimistic perspective makes it easier to control one's stress levels, which in turn enables one to save their vital energy and physical resources for times when they are required the most. Optimism has been demonstrated to strengthen a person's immune system, increase their ability to tolerate discomfort, and even speed up the healing process of wounds, all of which might be crucial in the event of a fight for survival.

The dynamic of the team

When traveling through the wilderness with a group of people, such as a family or a group of friends, maintaining group morale is extremely important. Children who are taught the value of always retaining a good attitude are valuable assets in the aforementioned circumstances. Their upbeat attitude may easily rub off on others, making it an effective rallying point for the group. Maintaining a positive attitude among the members of the group is important for several reasons, including the facilitation of improved communication, the promotion of collaboration, and the encouragement of innovative solutions to obstacles.

Finding Solutions to Deal with Fear and Uncertainty

The wilderness is notorious for its high degree of unpredictability. Confronting the unknown can result in feelings of anxiety and uncertainty, both of which have the potential to prevent action and impair judgment. Helping children face their concerns head-on can be facilitated by instilling in them the value of maintaining an optimistic viewpoint. Children acquire the attributes of bravery and resolve, which are needed in times of crisis, when they are taught that it is OK for them to be afraid, but that they must also comprehend the significance of understanding the value of pushing through their fears.

Developing Capabilities Necessary for Life

It is not simply about immediate survival, which is perhaps the most crucial reason to cultivate a happy mindset while one is in a wilderness area. It gives children a set of skills that may be applied in a variety of contexts throughout their lives. The mental skills that kids learn during their time spent in the wilderness will serve them well later in life, regardless of whether they are addressing scholastic problems, relational concerns, or any other kind of obstacles they may come across in the course of their lives.

In conclusion, a good attitude is more than simply an optional survival gear; it is an important component that compliments physical readiness and abilities. Having a positive attitude is an essential component that supports having a positive attitude is crucial. When kids are out in the wilderness, having a positive attitude may be both an instant lifesaving and a long-term life lesson for them. Understanding the power of positivity can be a lifesaver. Their experiences are enriched, they learn how to deal with adversity, and they are more prepared for the complexities of the adult world as a result of it.

Basic Wilderness Safety Tips

Children may develop a meaningful connection with the natural world, acquire useful new skills, and have a fantastic time by going on an excursion that takes place in the open air. The wild, on the other hand, is never predictable and always presents a new set of challenges. It is imperative that children (and the adults who are accompanying them) are aware of certain fundamental wilderness safety rules in order to guarantee that they have an enjoyable and risk-free time. The following are some pointers that should be kept in mind:

Prepare for the future

Planning ahead thoroughly is one of the first things you should do to keep everyone safe. Be sure that you are familiar with the location that you will be exploring, and never forget to let someone who isn't going on the trip know your plans as well as the approximate time that you will be back. In the event that something goes wrong, this individual can serve as a safety net for you. In addition to that, check the weather forecasts and be ready for any unexpected developments.

Dress in an Appropriate Manner

It's amazing how much of a difference it can be just to wear the appropriate clothes. Choose outfits that are made up of many layers and can simply be added to or taken off when the temperature shifts. It is extremely important to ensure that your outer layer is both waterproof and windproof, particularly when venturing into colder locations. In addition to that, you must have a robust pair of shoes or boots.

Bear in Mind the Necessities

Always make sure you have a basic survival kit on you, which should contain goods such as a first-aid kit, a map and compass, a torch with spare batteries, a multi-tool, and materials for lighting fires, such as waterproof matches. Bring along adequate amounts of both water and food, including high-energy snacks like granola bars and trail mix, just in case.

Hold fast to one another

The buddy system is especially important for young people who go on adventures. Children should never be alone and should be taught to stick close to one another at all times. Going off on your own can put you in potentially hazardous circumstances, such as becoming disoriented or coming into contact with wild animals.

Awareness of the Wildlife

When we talk about the wildlife, one of the most exciting things about being in the outdoors is having the opportunity to observe creatures in the environment in which they were meant to live. However, it is essential to keep in mind that the behavior of wild animals might be difficult to predict. Teach children to stay at a safe distance when seeing wild animals and to never approach them, feed them, or attempt to pet them.

Hydration as well as Sustenance

Because children do not always understand when they are thirsty or hungry, it is essential that they be reminded on a regular basis to consume water and food. In the bush, it's important to stay hydrated and keep your energy levels up because both of these factors can contribute to poor judgment and physical weakness.

Abilities in Navigation

Even while navigational aids like GPS are part of today's sophisticated technology, their dependability in more rural areas is not guaranteed. The ability to read a map and use a compass, among other fundamental navigational abilities, are extremely useful. Instruct children in these abilities and check that they have a fundamental comprehension level before taking them outside.

Be familiar with the fundamentals of first aid

In a time of crisis, even basic understanding of first aid may be of great assistance. Teach your children how to properly care for small wounds, what to do in the event of sprains or fractures, and how to identify the symptoms of diseases that are caused by extremes of heat or cold.

The Leave No Trace Principles should be followed

Not only can instilling in children a reverence for the natural world via adherence to the Leave No Trace principles safeguard the environment, but it also helps to maintain the stability and accessibility of hiking routes and camping areas. This includes correctly getting rid of rubbish, keeping campfire impacts to a minimum, and showing respect to both animals and other people who are there.

Kids may have a satisfying outdoor experience while reducing their exposure to potential dangers by adhering to some fundamental wilderness safety rules. The most important things are to be well-prepared, alert, and to have a healthy respect for the strength and unpredictability of nature.

Chapter 2

Preparing for Your Adventure

Recommended Gear for Young Explorers

It is essential to ensure that young explorers have the appropriate equipment in order to have a positive and happy time in the great outdoors. Having the appropriate gear may make all the difference between a vacation that is memorable for all the right reasons and one that is marred by pain or even risk. The following is a list of items that are recommended for use by young explorers when they are adventuring in the great outdoors.

Packing cubes

A backpack that is both well-fitted and comfy is an absolute need. Keep an eye out for straps that can be adjusted, a number of different compartments, and a design that appropriately distributes weight.

The size of the bag should be adjusted based on the duration and nature of the trip, but it should be roomy enough to carry all of the child's essentials without being unduly burdensome for them to carry.

Things to wear

When it comes to clothing for outdoor activities, layering is essential. A base layer that is made of a material that wicks away moisture helps to keep sweat away from the body. Insulation can be provided by a thermal mid-layer garment like a fleece jacket, and protection against the elements can be provided by an outer layer that is both waterproof and windproof. In addition, you should choose a solid pair of hiking boots or trail shoes, as well as socks of a decent quality that wick away moisture.

Kit de Premiere Aid

A standard first aid kit is an item that should always be on hand. Bandages, antiseptic wipes, tweezers, pain relievers that are appropriate for children, and any other personal medications should be included. Instruct the children on the correct way to make use of the objects.

A System for Hydration

It is essential to maintain proper hydration. It is helpful to provide children with water bottles, but a hydration reservoir (also known as a hydration bladder) can be an even better option since it enables children to drink water without having to stop and open a bottle each time, they want a drink. Make sure that the youngster will have an easy time manipulating whatever you decide to go with.

Food and drink

Trail mix, granola bars, and fruit leather are examples of high-energy, non-perishable foods that you should pack. If you are going on a longer journey, you might think about bringing camping cuisine that just needs hot water to be prepared.

Instruments of Navigation

Even if adults are guiding the route, it is still beneficial for young explorers to have their own set of navigation instruments, such as a map and compass, so that they may practice their abilities while being supervised. There are also GPS gadgets that are safe for children and meant to be user-friendly and long-lasting.

Multi-Use Device

A child-friendly multi-tool may come in useful for a variety of jobs, and it can also teach youngsters about the need of being resourceful. Make sure it has the essentials like tweezers, scissors, and a knife (if it's acceptable for the age group).
Sparking agent
It is possible to simplify the process of making a fire by using things such as weatherproof matches, a compact lighter, and fire-starting materials such as cotton balls soaked in petroleum jelly. This is a product that is intended for use by adults; however, older children may use it as a learning aid if they are well supervised.

Headlamp or other Type of Light Source

When going on a trip, it is important to bring along a tiny flashlight or headlamp, especially if you plan to be out after the sun has set. Pick one that has a range of dimmer settings, and don't forget to bring along some spare batteries.

Signal for Urgent Help

A simple yet efficient method of personal protection is the use of an emergency whistle. Instruct the youngsters that they should only use it in times that require their immediate attention.

Spray for insects and sun protection

It is essential to have protection from the sun and insects. Choose a broad-spectrum sunscreen with at least SPF 30 and an insect repellent that is appropriate for use on youngsters.

Notebook and Writing Instruments

The last thing that you should bring on your vacation is a small notepad and a pencil. You may use these items to jot down observations, draw pictures, or create a travel journal while you are away.

Having the right equipment improves your time spent in the woods by making it both safer and more comfortable. By taking the time to thoughtfully pick and pack gear that is tailored to the needs of young explorers, parents may help their children lay the groundwork for a lifetime of outdoor experiences.

Packing the Right Gear: A Checklist for Young Explorers

It may be both thrilling and nerve-wracking to get youngsters ready for an outdoor excursion or activity. Finding the right balance between ensuring that they have all they require and overpacking can be challenging. It is possible that having a checklist that is well-organized will make the procedure substantially simpler and more effective. The following is an exhaustive check list that has been curated specifically for young explorers who are going into the wilderness:

Things to wear

• The base layer should consist of t-shirts and long underwear that drain away moisture to keep sweat from sticking to the body.

• Insulating layers, such as fleece coats or sweatshirts for added warmth, make up the mid-layer.

• Jackets and pants that are watertight and windproof serve as the outer layer and provide protection from the elements.

• Underwear and Socks: A number of different pairs of wicking underwear and socks to keep moisture at bay.

• Hat and Gloves: A sun hat for situations that are warm and either a wool or fleece hat for environments that are cooler, combined with a pair of gloves.

• Footwear should consist of rugged hiking boots or trail shoes with a solid grip on the terrain.

Outdoor Equipment

• The child's backpack has to be able to be adjusted, provide comfort, and be the right size for them.

• Sleeping Bag: Appropriate for the season and temperature circumstances.

• When camping, a sleeping pad is used to provide insulation from the cold and hard ground.

• Tent or other form of shelter When camping for the night, it is necessary to bring along a tent that is not only portable but also simple to erect.

• Both Navigation and Communication are Included.

• Both the map and the compass should be laminated or placed within a watertight container.

• Whistle for Emergencies is lightweight and simple to use.

• Itinerary: One copy should be kept in the rucksack, and the other should be given to someone who is not going on the trip.

Hydration as well as Sustenance

• Water bottle or hydration system that is simple to carry and easy to refill.

• Snacks are high-energy items that do not need to be refrigerated, such as trail mix, granola bars, and dried fruits.

• Meals: If the vacation involves camping, pre-packaged camping meals or choices that are simple to make should be brought along.

Taking Care of Oneself and One's Health

• First Aid Kit: Specifically designed for children, containing items such as band-aids, antiseptic wipes, and medications that are safe for use in children.

• Sunscreen should have a broad-spectrum protection factor of at least 30.
• Insect repellent spray that is suitable for use around children.

• The greatest sorts of towels and washcloths are those that are compact and dry very quickly.

Equipment and Miscellaneous

• When purchasing a multi-tool, you should make sure that it is suitable for the child's age and that it has important tools like tweezers and scissors.

• Either a flashlight or a headlamp, as well as spare batteries.

• Firestarter is a combination of fire-starting material and matches that are water resistant. (Only intended for usage by mature individuals or under the direct supervision of an adult.)

• Use the notebook and pencil to keep a journal, draw pictures, or play educational activities.

• Camera: Not required, but recommended for documenting special moments.

Essential Items for Leave No Trace

• Soap made from renewable resources may be used to wash dishes and hands.

• Garbage Bags: Used for transporting any and all rubbish.

• A trowel can be used to dig a hole if it is necessary to dispose of human feces.

This travel checklist is meant to serve as a reference and can be modified to accommodate the unique requirements of the excursion, the time of year, and the area that you will be experiencing. Don't forget to get the kids involved in the packing process; it's a terrific chance for them to pick up valuable lessons about responsibility and being prepared. You are doing more than simply setting the stage for a pleasant and successful expedition when you prepare everything in great detail; you are also teaching young explorers essential life skills that will serve them throughout their lives.

Weather Forecast: Why It's Essential

Any activity that takes place outside is dependent on the weather for its success and safety, but this is especially true when children are participating. In spite of how much we might want to count on blue skies and ideal temperatures, Mother Nature has a tendency of surprising us with unexpected turns of events. Before venturing out into the wilderness, it is important to familiarize oneself with the local weather prediction in order to maximize the likelihood of having a positive experience while minimizing the risk of getting into a precarious one. The following are a few reasons why it is critical to keep up to date.

To Begin With, Safety

In the first place, it's important to keep in mind that the weather can quickly deteriorate from calm to severe, particularly in some regions of the world. Storms, gusty winds, high temperatures, and unexpected temperature decreases are all potential threats that should not be taken lightly. If you are aware of the forecast, you will be able to make appropriate preparations for the weather or, in certain situations, you will be able to reschedule your expedition. When children are involved, safety should always be the top priority; however, this should always be the case.

Preparation of the Gear

Different sorts of clothing and equipment are required for use in the different kinds of weather. A sunny forecast, for instance, may need the use of more sun protection, hats, and maybe even clothing that is breathable and lightweight in order to avoid being overheated. If, on the other hand, there is a chance of precipitation, then you will need to bring along rain clothing that is waterproof and rain coverings. If you keep an eye on the weather prediction, you'll be able to pack the gear that's most suited for the conditions, which will make the trip more enjoyable and protect your health.

Planning Future Events

The weather is another factor that determines whether activities are possible. In rainy weather, hiking paths can become quite hazardous due to their increased slickness, and windy conditions can make water-based sports such as kayaking potentially hazardous to participants. When you know what the weather is going to be like, you can plan activities that will allow you to have fun while keeping you safe from any potential hazards. This is something that might be especially crucial for younger explorers, who might not yet have the experience or skills necessary to adjust to surroundings that are more difficult.

Administration of Time

Throughout the course of a day, weather patterns frequently shift, and having an awareness of these shifts can assist you in more effectively managing your time. For instance, if it is forecast that there will be thunderstorms in the afternoon, you may make preparations to finish up whatever you were doing and find someplace safe to go before the weather worsens. Alternately, if the weather forecast calls for extremely chilly mornings, you can choose to put off the beginning of your day's activities until later in the day. If you are able to effectively manage your time during your wilderness excursion, you will be able to maximize your enjoyment of the experience while maintaining a high level of personal safety.

Responsibility and Academic Training

Another educational opportunity that may be taken advantage of is instructing children on the significance of weather forecasting. They get an appreciation for the might of the natural world and a comprehension of the responsibilities involved in organizing and carrying out a trip. It teaches children how to be responsible explorers in the future by teaching them to constantly take into account how the weather may affect their plans.

Preparedness for Emergencies

Last but not least, having an awareness of the current weather conditions might assist you in better preparing for unexpected events. In the event that bad weather is forecasted, for instance, you should be sure to bring additional supplies with you. These may include extra food, emergency blankets, and even, in the direst of circumstances, a satellite phone.

In conclusion, checking the weather prediction is not simply a quick step that you should do while organizing an outdoor adventure; rather, it is a crucial component of the preparation that assures the safety and enjoyment of all participants, particularly young explorers. By making it a consistent component of your preparation, you may reduce the likelihood of potential hazards, improve the efficiency with which you manage your time, and teach future generations of nature lovers a sense of personal responsibility and reverence for the natural world.

What to Do When Separate from Your Parent or Guardian

A terrifying situation that no one ever wants to find themselves in is one in which they become separated from a parent or guardian while on an outing in the woods. However, it is absolutely necessary for young explorers to be prepared for scenarios such as these, as taking the appropriate procedures can considerably raise the likelihood of a speedy and risk-free reunion. In the event that you become separated from your parent or guardian while adventuring in the great outdoors, the following are some recommendations to keep in mind:

Pause, reflect, and take in the scenery

The first thing you need to do is remain still. If you freak out and start running about aimlessly, you can get further away from your group, which puts you in more danger. Take several slow, deep breaths in order to calm down. Take a look around to become familiar with your surroundings. Make a note of any landmarks or other distinguishing characteristics that may assist you in describing your location in the future.

Keep your position

In most circumstances, remaining where you are is the most prudent course of action to take. It is likely that your parents or guardians will go back over their tracks to seek for you, and if you remain in the same location, it will be much simpler for them to locate you. Find a place that provides some protection from the weather but can still be seen from a distance.

Make some racket!

If you have access to a whistle, use it; the sound will go further than your voice will and will need less effort to produce. It is customary to signal for assistance by blowing a whistle three times quickly and forcefully. In the event that you do not have a whistle, you can also be useful by shouting out or making other loud noises. This is especially true if you hear searchers yelling your name.

Make Use of Signals

To draw people's notice, display flashy objects or wear bright apparel in a prominent area. If you have access to a mirror, you may utilize the sunlight that it reflects as a kind of communication. During the evening, a flashlight may do the same function. Making yourself more obvious to others will speed up your rescue.

Talk to each other

Now is the moment to make advantage of any two-way radios or phones that still have service that you may have. It would be helpful if you could provide as much information as you can about your surroundings. If there is no signal, shutting off or placing your phone in airplane mode will assist save battery life for when you might need it in the future.

Reduce your use of both energy and resources

It is a waste of your energy to aimlessly walk around. Take a seat and try to keep warm. Make use of whatever at your disposal to protect yourself from the cold ground and wind. Be frugal with both food and drink, but make sure you remain hydrated.

The bare essentials

If it seems like you'll have to wait for a significant amount of time, you should think about meeting your fundamental requirements. In the event that you have to use the restroom, dig a tiny hole with a trowel and then cover it back up once you're done. If you still have food, you should be careful to ration it. Consume water, but do so in measured sips to prevent dehydration from setting in too rapidly.

Keep a Good Attitude

When it comes to fighting for one's life, having a constructive mental attitude may make all the difference. Keep your spirits up by humming a tune, reciting something you've remembered, or even just having a conversation with yourself in which you reflect on pleasant past experiences.

Getting lost in the woods and becoming separated from a parent or guardian is a terrifying experience; but, if you are prepared and know what measures to follow, you may considerably improve your chances of being found promptly and securely. These recommendations are meant to provide young explorers with the expertise and self-assurance they require to deal with challenging circumstances in the most productive and safest manner feasible.

What to Do When Lost in the Woods

For young explorers who might not have a lot of practice making their way through natural environments, becoming lost in the woods can be a particularly terrifying experience. Even if prevention is the greatest strategy—you should never stray too far from your group, and you should constantly be aware of what's going on around you—unfortunate events might still take place. Here is what you should do if you become disoriented when hiking through the woods.

Make a Pausing Effort to Calm Yourself

Stopping is the first thing that must be done. To ease your nerves, take a few slow, deep breaths. In these kinds of predicaments, panic is your worst enemy since it might prompt you to make reckless choices that could make the situation much more dire.

Take Stock of Your Circumstances

Take a long, hard look at your surroundings. Do you recall any recognizable landmarks, such as a particular rock structure, stream, or trail? If you have been marking your route, which is a prudent habit in any situation, you should search for those markings to help you find your way back.

Maintain your current position

People who are lost often make the critical error of continuing on their journey in the mistaken belief that they would eventually locate their way home. Most of the time, doing so merely brings them further away from safety. If you remain in the same location, it will be much simpler for the people trying to save you to locate you. Find a place that has some cover but is still visible from a distance away.

Put out the distress call

Make a signal for aid using whatever you have available. It is commonly accepted that a distress signal consists of three loud blows on a whistle. If you don't have a whistle, you can either use your voice or the sound made by striking two sticks together. Place colorful clothes or other objects that are easily noticed in an open location to draw the attention of those who are searching for something.

Make the Most of Your Available Means

If you have a bag with supplies, you need to be careful about how you ration them. Eat a normal amount of food and drink an appropriate amount of water, and avoid wasting anything. If you have a flashlight, try to use it as little as possible in order to preserve the battery. You should immediately contact for assistance if you have access to a phone and there is service. If that is not the case, switch it off to conserve battery life for a time when it may be actually necessary.

Construct a Makeshift Home for Yourself

If it appears like you'll be in the woods for a while, especially when it starts to get dark or the weather becomes bad, building a modest shelter can help shield you from the elements and keep you comfortable while you're out there. Create a barrier between you and the elements by using branches, leaves, and any other items that are at your disposal.

Make sure that others can see and hear you

Make directional indicators that someone could use to find you. Rocks and sticks can be used to create big markings on the ground. If you have access to a mirror, you can utilize it to direct sunlight toward any aircraft or searchers that may be nearby. Continue to make noise at consistent intervals in order to aid searchers in locating you.

Maintain a Positive Attitude

Mental toughness is absolutely necessary in precarious situations. Try to have a cheerful attitude even if it's going to be challenging. Sing songs, reminisce about wonderful times in the past, or think about what you'll do once you're in a secure location. A healthy mental state can help you remain attentive throughout the day and increase your ability to make decisions.

Making Preparations for the Protracted Process

If it appears that you won't be located before sunset, you should be ready to spend the night in the wilderness. Stay put in your shelter, make sure you're warm, and keep sending out signals at regular intervals.

It is a terrible experience to become lost in the woods, but if you keep these suggestions in mind, you may substantially improve your chances of being discovered and of being safe. Your basic objectives are to make it simple for others to locate you by remaining in one place and producing noise, and to shield yourself from the elements by limiting your resource use and constructing a safe haven. You may boost your chances of making it back home safely by keeping a level head and taking preventative action.

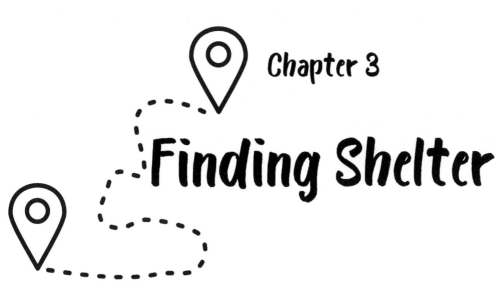

Chapter 3

Finding Shelter

The Different Types of Natural Shelters

Constructing a safe haven in the woods when you find yourself in a survival crisis is one of the most important things you can do for your own health and safety. The presence of shelter affords you protection from the elements, whether they take the form of rain, wind, cold, or even the sun. In this article, we take a look at the many kinds of natural shelters, namely, snow caves, trenches, and lean-tos or lean-to-like structures for locations that are mostly snowy or temperately wooded.

Lean-tos and Debris Huts

The construction of a lean-to, one of the easiest types of natural shelters to build, involves just a minimal amount of resources, most commonly simply a single lengthy branch to serve as the ridgepole and smaller branches or foliage to serve as the sides.

Components and Instruments:

• Branches or logs with sufficient length and strength for use as the ridgepole

• twigs that are less substantial or larger leaves.

• If cordage is available, use it.

The building trade:

• Find two trees that are sufficiently near to one another so that your ridgepole may go between them.

• The "lean-to" appearance may be achieved by propping the ridgepole against the trees at an angle.

• In order to construct a wall, prop additional, smaller branches up against the ridgepole at an angle.

• If you have access to it, a more effective barrier against the wind or rain may be created by using grass, leaves, or even mud.

The Good and the Bad:

• Rapid in construction

• Appropriate for use in less severe circumstances

• Not nearly as effective when up against severe conditions

Huts Made of Debris

Lean-tos are similar to debris huts, except debris huts are completely enclosed for increased safety. They need more time and effort to install, but provide superior insulation.

Components and Instruments:

• The ridgepole and the branches that support it.

• A substantial amount of leaves, grass, and tiny branches for use as covering and insulation.

• If cordage is available, use it.

The building trade:

• Begin with a ridgepole to create something that looks like a lean-to. But rather than keeping one side open, you should surround the other side with branches.

• Leaves and grass should be piled on both the sides and the top of the mound. The greater the thickness of the layer, the greater the insulation it will provide.

• Make an effort to construct an insulating layer on the ground if at all feasible.

The Good and the Bad:

• Superior insulating qualities

• It requires both time and effort to construct.

• Needs a lot of different materials.

Snow Caves and Trenches

Snow caves make for very effective shelter in snowy regions, but their construction requires a significant volume of snow and a lot of effort.

Components and Instruments:

• Consolidated snow

• Pick or use your hands

The building trade:

• Find a snowbank or a pile of snow.

• Start by digging in a horizontal direction, and then go upward to create a cave.

• Be careful to provide some sort of opening for air circulation.

The Good and the Bad:

• Superior insulating qualities

• requiring a lot of energy

• The possibility of failure in construction resulting in collapse.

The trenches

Snow caves are easier to construct than snow trenches, although snow trenches provide about the same level of protection.

Components and Instruments:

• Snow

• Pick or use your hands

• Skis or branches to use as a covering

The building trade:

• Create a hole in the snow that is wide enough for you to lie down in.

• Cover the top with skis, branches, or anything else that is level.

• If you have access to snow, piling it on top of the cover will provide further insulation.

The Good and the Bad:

• Rapid in construction

• Excellent for use as a makeshift shelter

• A snow cave provides more insulation than this.

Creating a Shelter with Materials at Hand

When you find yourself in a scenario where you need to survive in the wilderness, one of the first things you need to do is construct a shelter that will keep you safe from the elements. You may find that you do not have the luxury of a survival kit that is fully supplied on occasion, and you will be forced to make do with the things that are available to you. The following is a guide on how to construct a temporary shelter using whatever materials are at hand, regardless of whether you are in a forest, a desert, or an area covered in snow.

Take Stock of Your Circumstances

The first thing that should always be done is an assessment of what resources are easily accessible. Are there many branches and leaves to be found here? Do you have any snow? What about the very big rocks? The conditions of the surrounding area will determine the kind of protection you may construct. When attempting a rescue, it is important to take into consideration a variety of elements, including the direction the wind is blowing, potential water sources, and visibility.

Wilderness or a Wooded Region

Sticks, branches, and leaves are all things that are likely to be found in plenty in a forest. If you are able to locate a huge branch that has fallen over and broken off to serve as a ridgepole, you are off to an excellent start. Assemble the framework of a lean-to by securing this between two trees and leaning smaller branches against it to form the walls of the structure. You may add insulation to this structure by covering it with leaves, moss, or even dirt. This will also make it more resistant to water.

Environment like a desert

Large boulders and sand may both be utilized as key construction materials in a desert environment. Finding a huge rock formation in the desert and using it as a wall in your makeshift shelter is a straightforward approach to desert survival. After that, construct more barriers by placing smaller rocks or sand on top of one another. Finish it off by covering it with a makeshift roof constructed from old clothes, a tarp if you have one, or additional sand piles. To reduce how much, you are exposed to the weather, make sure the aperture is facing away from the wind.

Scenery that is Blanketed with Snow

When circumstances are snowy, you can make a snow cave or trench by digging into the snow itself. Begin digging with your hands, a stick, or a shovel if you have access to one ofthese tools. Digging through a snowbank and hollowing it out is the first step in making a snow cave. Create a trench by digging a ditch in the snow that is shallow yet long enough to lie down in. As a means of providing protection, you may cover the top with anything flat, such as branches, a tarp, or even your bag. Adding a layer of snow on top will provide further insulation.

Scenarios set in cities or after a catastrophe

Shelters can be made from recycled debris, such as huge pieces of cardboard, pieces of wood, or even metal sheets, in post-disaster or urban contexts. Always use extreme caution when it comes to the steadiness of the materials you are working with, especially if you are employing rubble from destroyed structures.

Maintain a Low Complexity

Building time will increase proportionately with the level of complexity of your shelter. Time is likely to be an essential component, particularly if you are attempting to beat the setting sun or an impending storm. It's better to have a shelter that's straightforward and well-built than one that's complicated and prone to collapse.

The Importance of Staying Warm and Dry

When you're trying to survive in the woods, being warm and dry isn't simply an issue of comfort; it's a matter of whether or not you'll make it out alive. Hypothermia, frostbite, and a lowered resistance to infection are just some of the serious health consequences that can result from prolonged exposure to circumstances that are extremely cold or damp. Your plan for survival will be guided by your understanding of the reasons for being warm and dry, which will affect your decisions on the construction of a shelter, clothing, and the management of resources.

The dangers of being wet and freezing

Hypothermia is a condition that occurs when your body loses heat at a rate that is greater than the rate at which it can create heat. At first, you can experience shivering, a feeling of confusion, or slurred speech. Your body may stop shivering as the condition develops, which is a sign that it is no longer able to warm itself by itself. This might finally result in the failure of all of the organs in the body and death.

Frostbite is a condition that can occur when skin that is exposed to extremely cold temperatures freezes. In the most severe cases, this may need the amputation of the affected limb.

A Decreased Immune System May Result from Cold and Wet Conditions Because these conditions exert stress on the body, resources are taken away from the immune system. Because of this, you are more likely to become unwell, which makes your current survival position much more difficult.

Keeping the Temperature Within the Core Stable

The optimal temperature for your body, measured at its core, is around 98.6 degrees Fahrenheit (37 degrees Celsius). The maintenance of this core temperature is essential for all of the body's processes, including the activity of the muscles, the digestion of food, and even clear thinking. When you are chilly and wet, your body needs to use additional energy in order to try to maintain this temperature. This results in rapid weariness and exhausted resources since your body's energy reserves have been spent.

Conserving Available Energy

Keeping yourself warm and dry is a good way to save electricity. In a precarious circumstance when your food intake may be severely limited or nonexistent, you will have a limited amount of energy to draw upon. The more energy you are able to save, the longer you will be able to keep up physical tasks such as looking for food or signaling for aid, and even the longer you will be able to keep your mind aware enough to make the prudent judgments necessary for survival.

Various Options for Clothing

Your first and most important line of defense against the weather is the clothing you wear. Having a number of layers that you can add to or take off in order to adjust to changing temperatures is great. Cotton, which loses its insulating capabilities when wet, is a material that should be avoided because it is preferred to use materials such as wool or some synthetics that give strong insulation and drain moisture away from the skin.

A Home and a Warming Fire

It is often required to construct a sturdy shelter and a fire in order to maintain one's heat and dryness. The combination of a well-built shelter that shields you from the wind and precipitation and a fire that provides heat and a mechanism to dry off wet gear is essential for survival. Even in circumstances in which it is difficult to be entirely dry at all times, it is necessary to have the ability to occasionally dry off.

Positive Effects on One's Mental State

Last but not least, one should not undervalue the effect that being warm and dry has on one's state of mind. Conditions that are cold and damp might be discouraging, which can increase emotions of hopelessness or terror. On the other side, having a fire to keep warm and clothes that don't get wet may substantially enhance your morale, which in turn improves your mental condition and, consequently, your odds of surviving.

Chapter 4

Sourcing Clean Water

Understanding the Importance of Hydration

In any precarious scenario requiring survival, keeping yourself well hydrated is of the utmost significance. Water is one of life's most essential requirements, and the significance of this fact is brought into sharper focus when one is struggling to survive in an undeveloped environment. The human body depends on water for everything, from cognitive function to physical endurance, and water is the linchpin that keeps everything together. In this article, we will discuss the importance of being hydrated, especially when it comes to the struggle for survival.

The Importance of Water to the Physiology of the Human Body

Within the human body, water fulfills a number of crucial functions, including the following:

Sweating and breathing are two of the ways that water contributes to the temperature regulation process that occurs within the body. This is absolutely necessary in precarious survival conditions in which you might be subjected to intense heat or cold.

Digestion: Water is an essential component of the digestive system, since it assists in the process of breaking down food in order to facilitate the absorption of nutrients.

Through the process known as circulation, oxygen and nutrients are delivered to cells, while waste materials are carried away by the blood, which is constituted largely of water.

Lubrication of the Joints: Water is essential for providing lubrication for the joints, which is necessary for mobility and is required in any kind of survival circumstance that calls for movement.

The Repercussions of Being Underhydrated

Decreased Physical Capabilities: A lack of water will almost immediately result in a decline in one's physical abilities. Muscles become more readily fatigued, and activities that were formerly quite easy become physically taxing.

Cognitive Impairment: The effects of even modest dehydration on a person's cognitive ability can be significant. The ability to make decisions, maintain attention, and remain vigilant are all impaired, which is particularly hazardous in precarious settings like wilderness survival, when every choice may have a direct impact on one's chances of surviving.

Dangers to One's Health: Severe dehydration can put a person at risk for life-threatening diseases such as heatstroke, renal failure, and even death.

The mental toll of being dehydrated might include increased irritability, anxiety, and depression. In a precarious scenario that requires you to survive, it is essential to keep a healthy mental condition in addition to good physical health.

Symptoms of Being Dehydrated

If you are able to identify the early warning symptoms of dehydration, you will be able to take preventative measures before the problem gets severe. Initial symptoms may include dry mouth, weariness, thirst, and urine that has a dark yellow color. As your condition of dehydration worsens, you may start to suffer symptoms such as dizziness, a racing heartbeat, and mental disorientation.

Locating and Cleaning Up the Water

Finding a trustworthy supply of water is of the utmost importance in the event that one must survive. Streams, lakes, and even the dew that forms on grass in the morning are all possible sources of water. On the other hand, purification is frequently required in order to remove microorganisms. One of the most trustworthy techniques is boiling the water, but if that is not an option, other options include the use of chemical purification tablets, water filtration systems, or even sun disinfection.

The Number Three as a Rule

According to the so-called "Rule of Threes" in the realm of survival, one may live for three minutes without air, three hours without shelter under harsh conditions, three days without water, and three weeks without food respectively. This highlights the crucial necessity of hydration, rating it higher than the need for food but somewhat lower than the requirement for urgent refuge from severe circumstances.

Ways to Find Fresh Water in the Wild

Finding a source of clean water is of the utmost importance in any situation involving survival in the woods. If you don't drink enough water, both your physical and mental functions will rapidly begin to degrade, making it increasingly difficult for you to make rational judgments or simply to move around efficiently. A talent that might save your life is the ability to discover water in different locations and know how to get it there. This guide will walk you through the process of locating this priceless resource in a variety of environments.

Waterways such as Streams, Rivers, and Lakes

Rivers, streams, and lakes are the types of water bodies that provide the simplest access to water. Because the flow of running water helps to lower the presence of germs and parasites, running water is typically considered to be safer than still water. However, before to ingestion, any and all-natural water sources should preferably be treated to eradicate germs by either boiling, filtering, or undergoing chemical treatment.

Rainfall

An approach that is considered to be generally risk-free for the acquisition of drinking water is the collection of rainwater. To collect rainwater, you can make use of any accessible container, such as cups, pots, or even leaves. If you have a tarp or a sheet made of plastic, you can use it to create a funnel that will collect water in a container.

Dew

Utilizing a cloth, you may use the early morning hours to collect dew that has formed on the leaves of plants. After removing the dew from the leaves with the towel by rubbing it across them, collect the liquid by wringing it out and placing it in a container. This technique requires a lot of work, but it can produce an unexpectedly large volume of water.

The Underground Water Supply

There is a possibility of water being found underground at times. The discovery of hidden sources can be made by digging a hole in a dry riverbed or at the base of hills and mountains. It is possible that water may seep up through the earth and fill the hole, providing you with a supply of water to drink. Keep in mind that you will still need to filter this water before using it.

Nature's greenery

There are certain plants that can supply water. For example, cacti are able to retain water in the stems of their plants. Some fruit-bearing plants and vines, in addition to bamboo shoots, have water in their tissues. However, you should use extreme caution since many plants contain toxins. Before turning to this strategy, it is recommended to have some familiarity with the flora of the local area.

Icy precipitation

Snow and ice are obvious sources of water in regions with colder temperatures. Always make sure they are melted before you consume them to prevent your core body temperature from dropping and putting you at danger for hypothermia. Never put your mouth directly on snow.

Environments Found Along the Coast

non spite of the fact that saltwater is inedible owing to the high concentration of salt non it, fresh water may still be found in coastal places. It is possible for there to be layers of fresh water floating on top of salt water in estuaries, which are the areas where rivers meet the ocean. Fresh groundwater that is rising to the surface with the tide can be uncovered by digging a few meters inland from the shoreline.

Animal Footprints

Animals, like humans, need water, and following an animal's tracks might help you find a source of water. Birds will frequently circle water sources, and the presence of swarms of insects may be an indication that water is close.

The Observation Deck and the Elevation Deck

In locations that are hilly or mountainous, travelling downstream or toward lower altitudes can frequently lead to the discovery of water sources. The lowest points of mountains and valleys are natural gathering areas for water.

How to Purify Water: Simple Methods for Kids

Maintaining proper hydration is an absolute must if you plan on venturing into the big outdoors. However, what should you do if the water you encounter does not appear to be very clean? There is no need to be concerned, since the following paragraphs will outline some methods that are not only simple but also appropriate for usage with children.

The simplest method is to boil the water

To make water safe to drink, one of the easiest and most reliable methods is to bring it to a boil. This is how you go about doing it:

Water Can Be Collected by Using A Container: You Can Use A container to collect water from a lake, river, or stream.

Use a cloth or your t-shirt as a pre-filter to remove any large debris such as leaves, sticks, or bugs.

Bring the water to a boil: With the assistance of an adult, bring the water to a boil for at least one minute over a campfire or on a portable stove. It's possible that you'll need to boil it for a bit longer if you're at a high altitude in the mountains.

Be sure to give the water some time to chill before drinking it.

The majority of the nasty microorganisms that might make you sick can be eliminated by boiling, making this method an excellent choice.

Utilization of Filters for Water

When they go camping, some individuals bring along portable water purification devices called water filters. These can be in the form of a pump or even a straw that the liquid is consumed through. They are capable of eliminating germs and even some of the tiniest viruses. Keep in mind that you should either read the instructions or ask an older person to demonstrate how to use the item.

Tablets or drops: it is the chemical treatment option

Tablets and drops designed specifically for the purpose of cleansing water are available. Make careful to carry out the steps in the manner they are outlined on the box, and if necessary, seek the assistance of an adult. Following the addition of the chemical to the water, you will need to wait for it to take effect for the allotted length of time.

Solar Water Purification: Harnessing the Power of the Sun!

Did you know that exposure to sunlight may help disinfect water? How to do it:

To begin, pour water into a bottle made of transparent plastic.

Shake It: To introduce some oxygen into the mixture, simply replace the cover and give it a good shake.

Put It in the Sun: Ensure that the bottle is exposed to direct sunshine for a minimum of six hours.

The flavor of the water will not improve in any way, but a good number of the bacteria should be eliminated.

The Bandana Way of Doing Things

You can use a piece of fabric or your bandana if you don't have any other tools or chemicals available to you. This will not destroy the bacteria, but it will remove things like mud and leaves off the surface.

Holding the fabric tightly over the mouth of a container will allow you to stretch the bandana.

Pour: Very slowly pour the filthy water into the container while the cloth is underneath it. It is important to keep in mind that even after utilizing the bandana approach, you should still make every effort to boil the water.

Important Reminders for Children

Always seek an adult for assistance, but this is especially important while handling boiling water or dangerous substances.

Even after you have attempted to clean the water, you should not drink it if it contains particles floating in it or if it smells strange. It's always better to be safe than sorry!
You now have some fantastic options at your disposal for ensuring that the water you find in the great outdoors is fit for human consumption the next time you embark on an excursion into the woods. Remember that staying hydrated is essential to having fun and maintaining your health when you're outside.

Chapter 5

Finding and Preparing Food

Recognizing Safe-to-Eat Plants

If you find yourself lost or trapped in the woods, it may be a terrifying experience; but, if you know how to feed yourself in this kind of situation, it can completely shift the game. Even if you might not be able to find a grocery store in the midst of a forest or a desert, it is not uncommon to come upon plants that could be used as food in those environments. However, you should not ingest every plant because some of them are known to be toxic or even lethal. Find out how to detect which plants are typically safe to ingest and how to carry out the Universal Edibility Test with the help of this guide.

Identifying Plants That Are Fit for Consumption

When it comes to determining which plants are risk-free to consume, there are a few fundamental rules to adhere to:

• Keeping an eye on the local wildlife is a good way to determine whether or not particular plants or fruits are fit for human food. If animals are seen eating them, it's a good bet that they are. Having said that, this approach is not 100% reliable because there are certain plants that are harmless to animals but harmful to people.

• Check for stench: A powerful, off-putting stench is typically a warning sign that something is wrong.

• Plants that have milky sap are dangerous and should be avoided at all costs since it typically contains toxins.

• Form of the Leaves: As a general rule, you should steer clear of plants that have leaves arranged in groups of three or that have leaves that are glossy or discolored.

• The color berry comes from an old proverb that reads, "White and yellow, kill a fellow." Beneficial to you are the colors purple and blue. Stick to fruits and berries that are typically regarded safe, such as blueberries or blackberries, even if this is only a general rule of thumb and isn't always correct. It's preferable to stick to fruits and berries that are generally considered safe.

• Consult a Guide: If you are in an area where there are edible plants, and you have access to a field guide to those plants, this is the most effective way to determine which plants are safe to consume.

The Universal Edibility Test

The Universal Edibility Test is a methodical approach to determining whether or not a plant may be consumed safely. Even if it takes a lot of time, it might save your life in a precarious scenario. The procedure entails a number of procedures, and it should only be carried out in situations in which there are no alternative viable food sources and when there is uncertainty regarding the plant's level of toxicity.

• Distinguish: Distinguish the plant into its fundamental components, which include its leaves, stems, roots, and flowers.

• Smell: An overpowering odor that is disagreeable is typically a warning indicator, as was discussed before.

• Skin Contact: Take a little piece of the plant and massage it on an area of your skin that is very sensitive, such as the inside of your wrist or your elbow. Hold off for a few hours. It is not safe to consume the plant if it causes your skin to become red, itchy, or irritated.

If the plant passes the skin test, the following step is to press it against your lips for three to five minutes in order to do the lip test. Do not consume the plant if you get any sort of burning or tingling sensations.

The next step in the process is to put the plant on your tongue and keep it there for 15 minutes if the previous step was successful. Avoid chewing or swallowing anything. If you have any kind of response to it, you should spit it out as soon as possible.

Chew Test: After the plant has been evaluated using the tongue, the next step is to chew it thoroughly but not to consume it. Continue waiting for the next 15 minutes to see if there is any reaction.

If you've made it this far without any adverse effects, the next step is to ingest the plant and wait a few hours after doing so. If you are experiencing any kind of pain, you should try to throw up and drink a lot of water.

• Observe: If you wait many hours without experiencing any adverse effects, it is likely okay to eat the plant in question. However, begin with a low quantity and gradually build up to the target amount.

• Repeat: Because the roots, leaves, blossoms, and stems of the plant can all have varying degrees of edibility, you will need to conduct this test many times for each section of the plant.

In order to survive, one must think creatively and act cautiously. There are parameters that may be used to identify safe plants; however, these recommendations are not 100% accurate. The Universal Edibility Test (UET) provides a more methodical strategy, but it should only be utilized in cases where no other options are available. Before consuming any strange plants or fruits in the field, young explorers should always seek the advice of elders or knowledgeable individuals. When it comes to surviving in the wild, it is imperative that one constantly errs on the side of caution rather than regret.

Basic Animal Tracking for Food

Finding food is one of the most important components of living in the wilderness, yet it is also one of the most difficult. Even if hunting is likely the first thing that springs to mind, young explorers may find that it is not always possible to engage in this activity. The tracking of animals, on the other hand, might bring you not only to prospective supplies of meat but also to other important resources such as eggs, honey, or even edible plants that animals like to feed on. The following are some fundamental pointers on animal tracking that may come in helpful at some point.

Acquiring Knowledge of Animal Signs

The first thing you need to do while tracking is to know what signs to look for. Direct and indirect animal indications can be distinguished from one another.

Direct evidence can be found in the form of trails, animal footprints, and feces (also known as animal droppings).

Indirect evidence includes chewed up leaves, scratching posts, tunnels, and nests. Nests can also be found in abandoned burrows.

Investigating the Tracks

You can learn a lot about an animal from its tracks, including its size, the direction it was traveling in, and even its speed.

Form and Measurement: The form and measurement of the trace can give you a decent indication of the species of animal that left it. The presence of hoof impressions is often indicative of a deer or elk, the presence of paw prints may indicate a small animal such as a raccoon, and the presence of huge padded prints may indicate a predator such as a cougar or a bear.

The depth of the trace might provide some insight on the size of the animal that left it. Pattern: The pattern of the tracks, including the distance between each individual trace, may be used to assist determine how fast the animal was moving.

Keeping an Eye on the Droppings

Even scat may reveal a lot about a person. What sort of animal it is and what it has been consuming may often be deduced based on its size, form, and the contents of its stomach? The droppings of herbivores often contain particles of plant material, whereas the droppings of carnivores typically contain fragments of bone or fur.

Animal Tracks and Hiking Routes

Many times, animals go along the same trails again and over again. These pathways are a wonderful spot to search for animal footprints and droppings, which may give you an indication of the kinds of animals that are roaming about the region.

Attend to the Sky and Hear

Don't limit your search to the ground; food may also be found in the trees and among animals that live there, such squirrels and birds. Pay attention to any sounds, like as calls, the rustling of leaves, or anything else that can help you pinpoint their location.

The Time of Day Is Crucial

Many kinds of animals are active at various times of the day. If you are able to learn the behaviors of possible food sources, it will be easier for you to determine when to monitor them. For instance, the dawn and sunset hours are often the times of day when deer are the most active.

To Begin With, Safety

It is essential to keep in mind that monitoring animals puts you in close proximity to dangerous creatures that might attack you. Always be aware of your surroundings, and make sure that you are well-equipped to deal with any creatures that may potentially be a threat to you.

Don't panic if you ever find yourself in a circumstance in which you need to make meals but you don't have access to contemporary cooking equipment like stoves or ovens. Fire, stones, leaves, and even dirt may all be used as ingredients in cooking techniques that have been around for centuries and have shown their effectiveness. In the event that you find yourself in a remote location, the following are some easy methods for preparing meals.

Cooking Over an Open Fire

Spit-roasting is perhaps the method that is the least complicated of the three. You'll only need a solid, long stick and a fire to get started. Insert the meat or fish inside the stick, and then turn it over the flames as you cook it. Be sure to turn it over at regular intervals so that it cooks evenly.

Coals in a Bed: After allowing your fire to burn down, you should be left with a bed of hot coals. Your meal should be wrapped in leaves and then placed directly on the fire to cook. This is an effective method for cooking meat in bite-sized bits or root vegetables.

Stone-Age Methods of Cooking

For a stone grill, place the stones in a circle around the fire and let them to get hot. After the stones have been heated, you may cook meat, fish, or vegetables by placing them directly on the stones.

Bringing Water to a Boil with Hot Stones: If you have a container that can hold water, such as a wooden bowl, but you are unable to set it over a fire, you can bring the water to a boil by using hot stones. Bring stones to a high temperature over the fire, and after they are ready, slowly place them in the water where your food is stored.

Oven made of clay or mud

To make an oven suitable for fish or meat, dig a small hole in the earth and line the bottom with stones. Your meal should be placed on the stones, and then a layer of dirt or clay should be placed on top of it. Construct a fire there, and allow it to blaze for a number of hours. The meal will be baked inside of the clay oven due to the heat.

Wrap your meal in a thick coating of mud and then set it on the coals of a fire to cook it. This is called a "mud wrap." When the mud has dried and cracked open, this indicates that the meal is ready to be eaten.

Condensing on the Leaves

Cooking vessels may be made from large, non-toxic leaves such as banana leaves and used to make leaf pouches. Put your meal in the leaf, fold it over, and fasten it with twigs to keep it from falling out. To cook the food, either position the bag so that it is close to glowing embers or suspend it over the fire.

Dig a shallow grave and line it with heated stones and leaves to use the leaf burial technique. On top of this, place your food, and then cover it with more leaves and dirt. The food will be cooked by the heat and the steam.

Cooking in Ash

Using this technique, you will first dig a small hole in the ground, then place your meal inside the hole, and last cover the food with hot coals and ash. When used for cooking root vegetables, it works really well.

Tips to Conclude

Always check to be sure the items you're employing are non-hazardous and safe. Some leaves, for instance, may contain toxins that are harmful to humans.

When working with hot stones or coals, exercise extreme caution. To protect yourself against burns, use sticks or tongs made from green wood rather than dried wood.

You will not only feel more connected to our predecessors, who utilized these techniques for millennia, but you will also develop vital abilities that might serve you well in a survival crisis if you are able to master these easy cooking methods. This is because our ancestors have been using these techniques for millennia.

Chapter 6

Navigating the Wilderness

Using the Sun and Stars for Direction

It may appear to be difficult to navigate through the wilderness without the assistance of modern instruments such as a GPS or compass; however, the sun and the stars really provide their own navigational markers, so there is no need to worry about getting lost. Learning how to interpret the movements and positions of these heavenly bodies can save your life and change a potentially hazardous scenario into one that is more controllable. Let's begin with the sun, which is the object in the sky that can be seen the most easily and immediately. The most important criterion for navigating during the daylight is that the sun always rises in the east and sets in the west. It is possible to make a rough approximation of the cardinal directions by watching the position of the sun. In the morning, as the sun is coming up, it indicates that you should

head toward the east; in the evening, as it is going down, it indicates that you should head toward the west. When the sun is at its greatest point in the sky, your position in relation to the sun determines the direction you are facing. If the sun is in front of you, you are facing south, and if it is behind you, you are facing north. Although it is not 100% precise, it is accurate enough to prevent you from getting lost or wandering in circles.

When the sun goes down, you may use the stars and other natural landmarks to help you orient yourself. The North Star, also known as Polaris, acts as a reliable compass that points in the direction of geographic north in the Northern Hemisphere. The North Star, or Polaris, is easy to find because it lies almost exactly perpendicular to the axis that defines the rotation of the Earth. You may discover Polaris by locating the Big Dipper constellation, which contains two stars forming the outer section of its 'bowl.' This will lead you to Polaris. If you were to imagine a line that went from these two stars to Polaris, it would take you there without any detours. The Southern Cross fulfills a role analogous to that of the Northern Cross in the Southern Hemisphere. It is made up of five stars, and when it is fully stretched, the long axis of the cross points towards the direction of the South Pole.

Even when night is cloudy and you can't see the stars, the moon can still help you find your way, but it will be more difficult. As you watch the moon as it transforms into a crescent, mentally draw a line that connects the points of the crescent and continues it all the way to the horizon. In general, this will point south in the Northern Hemisphere, whereas in the Southern Hemisphere, it will point north in the opposite direction.

Learning to navigate using these natural means is not only necessary for your own survival in the woods, but it also gives you a sense of immense agency. It establishes a very basic link between ourselves and the world around us, as well as with old human activities. We can determine our spot on the Earth below by gazing up to the sky. This transforms what may appear to be an unending and bewildering scene into one that is accessible and even welcome. You can learn to rely on the sun and the stars as trustworthy tools in your survival skill set, just as explorers and adventurers have done throughout the history of humanity. All you need is some practice.

Recognizing Natural Landmarks

Recognizing and making use of natural landmarks is an essential part of learning how to navigate in the wilderness. This is in addition to having a grasp of celestial markers such as the sun and the stars, which are used as guides. It might be a mountain range, a river, a particularly interesting rock formation, or simply a particular tree that stands out from its surroundings. Waypoints during a journey are natural landmarks that assist the traveler make sense of the surrounding environment and provide points of reference that can lead the traveler back to a safe location or in the direction of their ultimate destination.

For example, mountain ranges typically run in pretty regular directions, which might assist you in gaining a better understanding of the cardinal directions across a greater distance. Rivers and streams, in a similar fashion, often flow from higher altitudes to lower ones and frequently lead either to bigger bodies of water or to populous regions as they make their way downstream. Following a river downstream is a time-honored way for locating civilization, or at the very least, getting to a location where there is a greater chance of running across other people. Even on a smaller scale, individual rocks or groups of unusual trees may act as landmarks to help you mark your route or remember the way back to a base camp. This can be helpful if you are hiking or backpacking in an unfamiliar area.

However, it is not enough to simply be able to identify these landmarks; one must also be able to comprehend how to make use of them. For instance, if you are in the Northern Hemisphere, and you know that moss often grows on the north side of trees, then you have a hint regarding the direction you are facing when other approaches fail. The patterns of animal footprints can provide information about local water sources or natural channels that lead across difficult terrain if you take the time to observe them. Even something as simple as monitoring the flow of water might provide you with useful information. For instance, water tends to concentrate in low-lying regions, so these would be natural spots to go for if you were in need of hydration.

However, the ability to recognize natural features has applications well beyond simple survival. It teaches us how to interpret the landscape as a rich text that is full of information and connects us to the natural world around us. It is a talent that helps promote awareness as well as the ability to observe, which compels us to look beyond our current worries and become aware of the wider environment that surrounds us. This way of interacting with the natural environment is not only beneficial from a practical standpoint, but it also has aesthetic and even spiritual benefits, giving the participant a profoundly enlightening feeling of location and connection to the natural world.

Therefore, the capability to detect and make use of natural landmarks is not simply a survival skill; it is also a type of ecological literacy that attunes us to the nuances and intricacies of the area that we are traversing. You aren't just going to get better at navigating your way through the wilderness if you learn to recognize and make use of natural landmarks; you're going to become a part of the wilderness itself, tuned in to its rhythms and patterns, just like the generations of explorers and indigenous peoples who came before us. This is a skill that can be passed down from generation to generation. This ability not only adds to our toolset for surviving, but also to our fundamental understanding of what it is to be alive and a member of this complicated and wonderful world.

 # Making and Using a Basic Compass

Building a simple compass can be a lifesaving skill in the event that you become disoriented in the bush and do not have access to any contemporary navigational gear. Magnetic compasses were the primary navigational tool utilized by humans for a very long time until the development of GPS and electronic compasses. Making a simple compass is a lot easier than you might think, and it can be done with some basic materials that you could discover in nature or have on hand as part of your survival kit. If you want to make a primitive compass, you can do so with some basic materials.

To begin, you are going to need anything that can be magnetized, such as a needle or a piece of wire. You may generate a static charge by rubbing the needle against your clothes or your hair. If you happen to have access to a magnet, that's fantastic; simply run the needle over it a few times. After that, you are going to have to float the needle. This may be accomplished in a number of different ways. If you have a leaf and some still water, you may put the leaf on the water, and then put the needle on top of the leaf. This will cause the needle to float to the surface of the water. You should be able to float the leaf, and the needle will naturally align itself along the north-south axis. This will provide you with a basic but functional compass. It is possible to use a little piece of paper or even a sliver of wood as a replacement for a leaf if you do not have access to one. If you are in the vicinity of a puddle or a pond, that is ideal; but, if you are not, you can hold the water in a cup or in your hands instead.

How exactly do you interpret the readings on this improvised compass? Because you magnetized one end of the needle, it will now point in the direction of magnetic north. In order to verify the reliability of your compass, you may compare its readings to those of the sun or the stars, provided that you are able to do so. After you have established the cardinal directions, you may navigate through the wilderness by using natural landmarks such as mountains and rivers to keep you on track with your destination. In addition, keep notes of these landmarks either in your head or on paper so that you don't end up going in circles or being even more bewildered.

However, the value of a simple compass extends well beyond its ability to simply indicate the direction of north; it may also serve as a tool for developing greater independence and self-assurance. The vastness of the forest seems to have suddenly become a bit less intimidating and a little more manageable. The psychological benefit of having a directional instrument should not be underestimated, even though the needle and leaf compass is not as exact as current alternatives. It provides a tangible sensation of control, which acts as an antidote to the fear that might set in when a someone is lost.

It's not only a great survival trick to be able to make and use a simple compass; it's a reflection of our intrinsic ingenuity, an embodiment of the human desire to travel, explore, and survive. Therefore, the skill of producing and utilizing a basic compass is more than simply a cool survival trick. It establishes a link between ourselves and a history of adventure that extends back millennia, to a period when our ancestors wandered undiscovered areas, guided by the stars, landscapes, and basic tools. By becoming proficient in this ability, you are not only navigating your way through the environment, but you are also tapping into a fundamental aspect of what it is to be human: the aspect of the adventurer and the survivor.

Chapter 7

🔥

Fire Building Skills

The Basics of Fire Safety

In the wild, fire may serve a variety of purposes as a tool. It keeps you warm, allows you to cook food, and may even be used to signal for aid. However, fire is also hazardous, and it must be managed in a responsible manner in order to prevent it from becoming a risk. Understanding the fundamentals of fire safety is not just a good idea; it is a necessary skill set for anybody who plans on heading into the great outdoors. This is especially important for younger explorers who may not be as knowledgeable about how quickly a little fire can become out of control.

It is crucial to select an appropriate site for your fire before you even think about lighting the match. To achieve the best results, the location should be free of any combustible substances, such as dead grass, leaves, or wooden constructions. It is in your best interest to clear a perimeter around the location you have picked for the fire, getting rid of everything that may possibly catch fire. Also, take into account the direction that the wind is blowing to ensure that the fire does not spread to your camp or any other locations that may catch fire.

After you have determined that the location is suitable, building a fire ring is a prudent next step to take. This may be accomplished by placing boulders around the perimeter of the space, which will serve as a barrier to keep the fire under control. If you happen to be in the vicinity of a body of water, you should keep some water on hand in case you need to put out the fire. In the event of a crisis, it is also a good idea to keep a nearby pile of soil or sand handy in case you need to use it for the same reason.

When it comes time to actually start the fire, you'll want to make sure that all of the necessary components, including tinder, kindling, and fuelwood, are well-organized and close at reach. Start by lighting the tinder, then add larger pieces of wood one at a time until you have a fire that is steady. If you want to start a fire, you should never use combustible substances like gasoline or alcohol since doing so might result in flames that are out of control and could cause injury.

After you have started a fire, it is imperative that you keep an eye on it at all times. Under no circumstances should you walk away from a fire, even if it seems to be blazing slowly and slowly. Because of the ease with which fires may spread, whether by being blown by the wind or grabbing onto stray items, even a contained flame can quickly become a dangerous wildfire. In addition, use extreme caution if adding extra wood to a fire that is already burning. If you want to prevent getting burned or causing embers to fly out of the fire, stand at a safe distance and throw the wood onto the flames.

When it comes time to put out your fire, it is really necessary to do it completely. The embers, the coals, and the sticks should all be soaked in water before proceeding with the fire. To ensure that everything is completely wet and icy to the touch, stir what is left over. In the event that you do not have access to water, you can put out the fire by smothering it with soil or sand; however, you must ensure that you mix the material thoroughly so that all embers are extinguished. Never put leaves or grass on top of a fire since both of these things might smolder and cause the fire to restart later.

Learning the fundamentals of fire prevention and protection is an essential component of any survival handbook for the wilderness. In a precarious circumstance, a fire may very well be your best ally; nevertheless, if it is not controlled properly, it also has the potential to become a destructive force. You may reap the advantages of fire without putting your own safety at risk if you have the right information and pay attention to what you're doing. This will ensure that your time spent in the outdoors is both fun and risk-free.

Collecting Firewood and Kindling

To begin, it is of the utmost importance to make a distinction between fuel, kindling, and tinder. The primary source of fuel is known as firewood, which is often made up of bigger logs as well as branches. The next stage is to use kindling, which consists of tiny branches and sticks that are used to assist light the larger pieces of fuel. Tinder is the flammable material that is used to create the first spark in a fire. Examples of tinder include dry grass or leaves.

Specifications for the Optimal Kinds of Firewood

When collecting firewood, it is essential that the wood be dry. Wood that is damp or still green will not burn well, if it ever burns at all. Keep an eye out for dead branches that are still hanging from trees; they are likely to be in a drier state than those that have fallen to the ground. Additionally, the wood should be seasoned, which means that it should have been dormant and been allowed to cure for a considerable amount of time. Hardwoods such as oak, hickory, or maple are fantastic for maintaining a fire for an extended period of time, but they can be more difficult to light.

The Significance of Stoking the Fire

The tinder on one end and the primary fuel on the other are connected by the kindling in the middle. It must be dry and somewhat thin, so that it may catch fire rapidly but continue to burn for a sufficient amount of time to light larger logs. The use of tiny bits of wood, such as twigs and branches, is typically recommended; however, bigger pieces of wood that have been cut down into smaller portions are also an option. Don't scrimp when it comes to kindling since starting a fire with it is really necessary.

Finding a Source of Good Tinder

Many types of natural materials can be used as tinder in an emergency situation. Leaves, grass, and pine needles that have been allowed to dry out can all be useful. Some people even make use of the fluffy "down" that may be harvested from plants such as cattails and milkweed. Tinder may be made out of wood shavings that are very fine or even the lint from your pocket if you are in a very dire scenario. In order to successfully light your kindling, the key need is that the material readily ignites in the presence of oxygen.

Putting Away and Making Ready

After you have amassed all of your resources, it is in your best interest to keep them organized. When it's time to start a fire, you'll want to make sure that your tinder, kindling, and fuel are kept in distinct locations so that you can quickly find what you need. If you plan on being in one location for a lengthy amount of time, it may be advantageous to construct a small shelter in order to keep your firewood dry, particularly if precipitation of any kind is anticipated, such as rain or snow.

Warnings and Precautions

When you are gathering firewood and kindling, make sure to use caution. Do not risk injuring yourself by attempting to break huge branches that are located over your head since they might fall on you. When utilizing cutting implements like knives or hatchets, always be sure to cut away from your body. Avoid collecting wood from locations that look like they may be animal homes or that are close to potentially dangerous terrain, such as cliffs or rivers that are moving quickly.

The process of constructing a fire is a lot more likely to be successful if you have a good understanding of how to correctly collect firewood and kindling. Not only does this make the work more manageable, but it also greatly enhances your odds of doing so. In return, that fire has the potential to become your savior by providing you with light, warmth, and a means to prepare food and clean water. As a result, this ability is more than simply a camping hack; rather, it is an essential component of surviving in the outdoors.

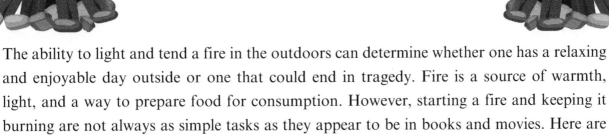

Simple Techniques to Start and Maintain a Fire

The ability to light and tend a fire in the outdoors can determine whether one has a relaxing and enjoyable day outside or one that could end in tragedy. Fire is a source of warmth, light, and a way to prepare food for consumption. However, starting a fire and keeping it burning are not always as simple tasks as they appear to be in books and movies. Here are some straightforward solutions that should assist you out.

The Groundwork: Getting Your Fire Pit Ready to Use

It is imperative that a proper fire pit be prepared before even thinking about starting a fire. This area has to be cleaned of any combustible objects, such as leaves or grass, before it may be used. To best control the spread of the fire, construct a ring out of rocks. This will not only assist you in maintaining control of the fire, but it will also serve as a reflector, bringing the heat closer to you.

First Step: Scattering the Matches

The item that will catch fire initially and contribute to the ignition of the kindling is called tinder. It might be anything, from paper to dried leaves to the bark of a tree. Place the tinder you have selected in the bottom of your fire pit. Make sure the material is dry before you try to light it, since else it will be impossible.

The second step is to stack the kindling.

Smaller twigs and sticks are what make up kindling in a fire. These will become engulfed in flames from the tinder, which will then spread to the larger logs. Build a tepee out of the kindling and place it on top of the tinder. Create some room for air to circulate around the fire, as oxygen is essential for the flames.

The third step is to add firewood.

As soon as the smaller logs and kindling are on place, you may go on to the larger ones. These should be stacked in a structure like to a cabin around the kindling, leaving room in between each layer for air to flow. Again, you need to make sure that these logs are completely dry before you try to light them. If the wood is damp or still green, it will generate a lot of smoke but not much fire.

Ignition is the fourth step.

At this point, you are able to start your fire. Start a fire in the tinder by striking a match, using a lighter, or igniting a fire starter. Blow on the base of the fire in a soft, even manner to supply it with additional oxygen, which will assist it in catching the kindling.

Maintenance is the fifth step.

After you have built your fire, the next important step is to keep it going. Maintain a vigilant watch over it and add logs as required. Be sure to store your firewood in logs of progressively bigger sizes; add smaller logs first, and then larger ones, to maintain a powerful and steady fire. If you add too many logs at once, you run the risk of smothering the fire. In addition to this, you should never walk away from your fire.

The sixth step is putting out the fire.

Take your time and be careful while putting out the fire when the time comes. It should be doused with water and the ashes should be stirred to ensure that every ember has been extinguished. Before you leave the scene, use the back of your palm to test the temperature of the ashes to make sure they are cool.

When it comes to a fight for survival, fire is not only a useful instrument but also a big duty. Always be sure to follow the requirements for fire safety, and never walk away from a fire unattended. Because you are able to light and manage a fire using these straightforward methods, your time spent in the great outdoors will not only be more pleasurable but also more risk-free.

Chapter 8

Signaling for Help

Creating a Signal Fire

In the outdoors, you can find yourself in a position where you need to call for assistance. The use of a signal fire is an extremely efficient approach to draw attention from a distance, whether it be from search and rescue teams or from planes in transit. A signal fire, as opposed to a standard campfire, is intended to produce a substantial quantity of smoke and flames in order to draw attention to yourself and others in the area. The construction of an efficient signal fire may be broken down into the following phases and suggestions.

The building, the neighborhood

When setting up a signal fire, the location is the

most important factor to take into account. Since visibility is the objective, the higher terrain is desirable. Remove any overgrown vegetation that may be in the way, and search for a location that provides a direct line of sight to the sky and the surrounding region. However, keep in mind that safety is of the utmost importance; while lighting your signal fire, make sure not to set it too close to dry grass or leaves, as this might spark a wildfire.

Things That You Will Require to Have

Tinder, kindling, and firewood are the fundamental components that must be present in order to start a fire; however, you will need many more of them. You will also want "smoke fuel" such as green leaves or branches, moss, or even things made of rubber or plastic that, when burned, make thick, colorful smoke. Maintain the separation of these items while making sure they are easily accessible.

Establishing the Framework for the Signal Fire

Construct a traditional fire pit with tinder, kindling, and fuel. Nevertheless, you should make it more robust than a typical campfire. The "pyramid structure" is an efficient design that requires stacking logs of progressively bigger diameters one atop the other in the form of a pyramid. This guarantees that the fire will continue to burn for a longer period of time and produces a more significant volume of smoke.

Ignition in addition to Timing

Before you start the fire that will serve as your signal, be sure you have the means to keep it going. Make sure that you have sufficient firewood and smoke fuel by checking your supplies. This will allow you to keep the flames and smoke at a high level. To get the tinder going and the fire started, you can use any source of ignition you have available, such as matches, a lighter, or a fire starter. In the early stages of the fire's development, when the flames are still relatively small, add your smoke fuel to produce dense clouds of smoke.

Upkeep in addition to Supervision

The signal flames demand your whole attention at all times. Keep an eye on the way the wind is blowing to ensure that your fire can be seen from above and does not represent a threat to the surrounding area. Be ready to add wood on a frequent basis in order to keep the fire running. If it is at all feasible, you should set many signal fires in a pattern like a triangle or a straight line. This will make it easier for people in the air to recognize the pattern as a signal of trouble.

Putting Out the Fire That Is Your Signal

Be sure to put out the signal fire in a meticulous and thorough manner in the event that your rescue is successful or in the event that you are forced to depart your site. You may extinguish the flames and embers completely by using water, earth, or sand. Always double check by touching the area (carefully!) to ensure that there are no embers left over.

A crucial ability that might potentially save your life in a precarious circumstance is the ability to build a signal fire. However, with this privilege comes the obligation of ensuring that it is carried out in a secure manner so as to prevent the start of unplanned wildfires. When starting a signal fire, you should always be prepared and aware of the conditions that currently exist in the surrounding surroundings.

Using Mirrors and Shiny Objects

When you are in a position where you need to survive, especially when you are lost or trapped in the woods, the most important thing you can do is send a signal for aid. While fire and smoke are useful for communicating over great distances and at night, reflecting surfaces such as mirrors and other sparkling things may be quite useful during the day. They attract and reflect sunlight in a manner that is difficult to ignore, which makes them fantastic instruments for catching the attention of those who are trying to help you.

The Scientific Justification for Reflection

A focused beam of light is produced when light strikes a surface that is both smooth and reflective. This causes the light to bounce back almost flawlessly. A diffused reflection, on the other hand, is produced when light strikes a rough surface and scatters in various directions. This is not the same thing. Because the focused beam produced by a mirror or other shining object is simpler to spot from a greater distance, these kinds of objects are preferred for use in signaling purposes.

Various Categories of Reflective Materials

If you have access to one, a signaling mirror is the most effective instrument for the task at hand. On the other hand, a great number of commonplace products can also suffice in a pinch. These are the following:

• Mirrors in the form of compacts or fragments of broken mirrors

• The reflective layer that may be found on CDs and DVDs.

• A buckle for a belt that is sparkling.

• A can lid or tin lid that has been polished.

• Foil made of aluminum

Signaling Method: Flashing the Lights

The "flash" approach is the most efficient way to make use of a reflecting surface for the purpose of signaling. To accomplish this:

• Aiming: While holding the reflecting item in one hand, extend the other arm and make the letter V with your fingers on the extended arm. Put your objective (such as a flying airplane or a hiker in the distance) in the crook of your index and middle fingers.

• Adjustment: Move the mirror (or any other things that are reflecting) such that the sunlight shines onto the hand that is forming the "V" symbol.

• To flash: Tilt the mirror ever-so-slightly to point the beam through the V and in the direction of your intended target. They need to be paying attention to the sudden flash of light. If it is at all practicable, you should make use of an already defined signaling code such as three flashes occurring in rapid succession.

Both the Length and the Recurrence

When employing reflecting signals, consistency and repetition are quite important. Check the object's location at regular intervals to make sure it is still in the right position in relation to both the sun and the goal. By flashing your signal at consistent intervals, you will increase the likelihood that it will be noticed.

Warnings and Precautions

While you are signaling, it is important to be aware of your surroundings. Be careful not to accidentally poke your eyes or the eyes of anyone who may be close with the focused beam of sunshine. Also, bear in mind that reflecting signaling is normally only effective during daytime hours and when the sky is relatively clear. This is something you should keep in mind.

Mirrors and other reflective items are easy to transport and don't take up much space, but they may be quite useful in an emergency situation. Learning how to utilize them effectively will dramatically boost both your visibility and the likelihood that you will be rescued. Practice is the best way to master any survival skill, so get acquainted with these strategies before you find yourself in a predicament in which you have to put them to use.

Making Noise:
Whistles, Clapping, and Shouting

Being lost in the woods or stuck there may be a terrifying experience; but, having the capacity to successfully signal for help can make all the difference in the world. Even though visual cues like as flames and reflected objects are extremely important, they are not always sufficient on their own. An auditory signal, such as a whistle, clap, or yell, can be more successful than a visible signal in some situations. This is especially true in deep woodlands or foggy circumstances, when visual signals may not be observed.

Why Sound Transmissions Are Effective

Sound may travel not just through air and water but also through solid things. In wide-open spaces like the wilderness, sound has the ability to travel significant distances and can draw the attention of anybody who is nearby. The more piercing and loud the noise, the greater the likelihood that it will be heard above the sounds of nature, such as the wind, the river, and the noises of the animals. In addition, a loud and unusual sound, such as a whistle or a yell, is immediately identifiable as an indication of the presence of a human being.

Instruments for the Production of Noise

The use of whistles

A survival whistle may be little, but it packs a powerful punch when you're out in the woods. It is loud, it can be heard across large distances, and it uses less energy than yelling would have done. Because of this, a whistle is a common item seen in survival kits. A signal of distress that consists of three brief bursts is understood on a global scale.

The act of clapping

Making noise with your hands clapped together is another option. Even if the sound is not as loud or as far-reaching as a whistle, it is still recognizable and may be used as a fast method to catch someone's attention. It also has the benefit of being "hands-free," which means that you do not require any additional equipment to use it.

A loud yelling

Shouting can appear to be the most basic way, but it really has several restrictions. It's possible that shouting will wear you out, and it won't be as loud as a whistle. Adding your voice to your auditory signals, on the other hand, may help express a sense of urgency and may carry an emotional weight that a clap or whistle cannot.

Techniques and timing that are appropriate

The use of whistles

Make as loud of a sound as you can while holding the whistle in your lips. If there is an emergency, you should indicate it using a rhythmic pattern, such as three short blasts.

The act of clapping

Make a resounding and forceful clapping sound with your hands. In a manner analogous to that of the whistle, you should try a pattern that sticks out, such as three quick claps followed by a pause.

A loud yelling

If you do want to yell, make sure that you are audible and clear. Random screaming might not be the most effective way to express your predicament, but yelling "HELP!" or "SOS!" might be.

Concerning Safety and Other Precautions

Although noise is beneficial, it also has the potential to warn animals of your presence. Although wild animals would often stay away from humans, you should constantly be mindful of your surroundings just in case. In addition, hearing impairment can be caused by disturbances that are both loud and continuous. Make limited use of your loudest signals, and only do so when you feel there is a strong probability that someone may hear you in the scenario you are in.

Your hands, your voice, and even something as simple as a whistle may be extremely effective means of calling for assistance in a time of need. Each has some advantages and disadvantages, but when utilized strategically and in conjunction with one another, they significantly boost the likelihood that you will be located. You should always have a whistle with you as part of your basic survival kit, and you should never underrate the power of your own voice or hands to warn others to your presence.

Chapter 9

Dangerous Animals and How to Avoid Them

Understanding Wildlife Behavior

The possibility of coming face to face with wild animals is one of the things that makes spending time in natural settings so exciting. Our interactions with wild creatures, such as bears and deer, as well as the innumerable species of birds, reptiles, and insects, bring an additional dimension of depth to the richness of our time spent in nature. However, having an awareness of animal behavior is essential not just for your own protection but also for the health and happiness of the other living things you come into contact

Why Should We Understand the Behavior of Wildlife?

It is vital, for a variety of reasons, to have an understanding of the usual habits of wildlife: Certain animals have the potential to be dangerous to people if they feel threatened or if they are confined in some way. If you are able to correctly understand their signals, you will be in a better position to respond accordingly.

Animal Welfare Getting too close to animals, which can cause stress, or guiding a predator to a vulnerable species can all be ways in which humans unintentionally do harm to animals.

Conservation: Engaging with animals in a way that is appropriate and respectful helps larger conservation efforts by reducing the amount of effect humans have on natural environments.

Common actions and behaviors of wildlife

Positions of Defensiveness

When they perceive a threat, many different kinds of animals engage in particular defense responses. Some animals, such as bears and rattlesnakes, may stand on their rear legs, and some birds can even puff up their feathers in response to a threat. If you are able to recognize these cues, it will be easier for you to give the animal the space it needs.
Pairing off and setting up home

When it is time for mating, many animals exhibit increased levels of hostility and territoriality. For instance, male elk and deer are notorious for the behavior known as rutting, which can be risky if you approach too near to them during this time. In a similar vein, certain animals, such as birds, are extremely protective of their nests and will fight to defend their young if they believe they are in danger.

Consumption Patterns

The different ways in which animals consume food can have an effect on the way you interact with them. Some animals are more active during the day (diurnal), while others are more active during the night (nocturnal), and yet others are most active during the early morning and late evening hours (crepuscular). If you are aware of the times of day when certain animals are most likely to be feeding, you can prevent inadvertent run-ins with them.

Advice Useful for Protecting Yourself

Maintain a courteous Distance: When with wild animals, you should always maintain a safe and courteous distance. When doing observation, use binoculars.

Store Food Properly: If you are camping in an area that is frequented by bears or other large creatures, you should hang your food high in a tree or use bear-resistant containers to store your food. This will prevent animals from coming to your campsite.

Travel in Groups: Larger groups have a tendency to produce more noise, which might alert animals to your presence and allow them a chance to avoid you. If you travel in groups, you reduce the likelihood that animals will attack you.

Be additional Cautious at Dusk and Dawn: This is when many animals are at their most active, so you should take additional precautions at these times.

The enjoyment of the great outdoors may be made more gratifying by gaining an understanding of the behavior of animals, which can also enrich our experiences and ensure that we can cohabit peacefully with the species who make these areas their home. To ensure that people and animals can safely coexist in these natural areas, just a little bit of education and a healthy dose of respect may go a long way toward achieving this goal.

Safe Distances and Respect for Wild Animals

The untamed splendor of the wilderness and the sense of seclusion it affords are frequently at the heart of the wilderness' appeal. On the other hand, we are not the only people that call these natural environments their home. When we go out into the wilderness, it is vital to keep in mind that we are visitors in their territory because wildlife plays such an important part in maintaining the health of the environment. The maintenance of a respectful distance from wild animals is not only a matter of common decency; it is essential to the health and happiness of both people and animals.

Why Do You Need to Keep Your Distance?

Protection of People

Animals can't be predicted in any way. When they feel trapped, frightened, or provoked, even people who appear to be innocent can become dangerous and represent a threat. Even though smaller animals, such as raccoons and even birds, might spread illnesses, larger species, such as bears, elk, and moose, are more likely to inflict severe harm.

The Well-Being of Animals

The presence of humans in their environment can make wild animals feel stressed and anxious. It is also possible for them to become used to the presence of humans, which can result in a dependence on the food provided by humans and a reduction in their ability to survive. Animals that have developed an unhealthy dependence on people are frequently referred to as "nuisance animals" and may either be rehomed or put to death.

Instructions for Maintaining a Safe Distance

The 'safe distance' might change based on the species, however the following are some common rules to follow:

At least one hundred yards away from large predators like bears, cougars, etc.

At least fifty yards away from medium-sized mammals such as deer, elk, and other similar animals

At a distance of at least 25 yards, small mammals and birds.

Animals that are Nesting or Mating: Maintain an even greater distance and try to avoid the area if at all feasible.

Suggestions for Keeping Boundaries Respected in Your Relationships

Equipment such as Binoculars and Zoom Lenses

Through the lens of a camera or a pair of binoculars is one of the most enjoyable ways to experience nature and its inhabitants. This enables you to see animals in great detail without having to get too physically near to them.

Watch Out for the Infant Animals

Young animals often have a lower level of fear when it comes to people, but their moms are typically close by and can get belligerent if they feel that their young are in danger. Always use extreme caution if you find yourself in an area where young animals are present.

It Is Unkind to Feed the Wild Animals

The practice of feeding animals may cause them to congregate closer to human settlements, which might increase the risk of dangerous encounters and automobile accidents. Additionally, it interferes with their normal nutrition, which might result in a variety of health problems.

Make a Move to the Side

If you find yourself unexpectedly near to an animal, you should walk laterally instead than straight backwards to get away from it. The majority of animals will see this as less dangerous, and it will typically urge them to move away from the area as well.

Our desire to explore the environment should be balanced with the requirements that the creatures who live there have for their habitat, and the best way to do this is to keep a safe distance from wild animals. It preserves their natural behavior and the cycles of their lives while also reducing the danger to human beings. By respecting these limitations, we are able to contribute to a happy coexistence, which in turn enhances our time spent in the wilderness and ensures that these breathtaking landscapes are preserved for future generations.

What to Do If You Encounter a Predatory Animal

The wilderness is home to a wide variety of flora and fauna, including dangerous animals such as bears and wolves. It's not often that you run across predatory creatures like bears, wolves, or mountain lions, but when you do, it may be an exciting and sometimes life-threatening experience. If you are prepared for these kinds of scenarios, you will be able to tell the difference between an interesting animal encounter and a potentially life-threatening crisis.

The Various Kinds of Dangerous Creatures You Could Run Into

Your current location will determine the specific predatory creatures that you may come across during your travels. These might be found in North America and include:
Bears: Grizzly bears as well as black bears and other varieties of bears

Cougars and pumas are both other names for mountain lions.

Although they are uncommon, wolves are sometimes spotted in certain regions.
Coyotes are often less dangerous than wolves, although they may still be hostile.

Prior to Your Trip, Take the Necessary Precautions

Before venturing out into the bush on any kind of journey, you should do some research on the many kinds of dangerous creatures you may run into and study how they behave. Bear spray is an important piece of safety equipment to have on you, and you should know how to use it. Never go anywhere alone without telling someone where you're going and what time you expect to be back.

What You Should Do in the Event of an Encounter

Don't Panic!

It's probable that your initial response may be terror, but you should try to keep as much composure as you can. The animal may become agitated if you make sudden movements or make a lot of noise.

Consider the Circumstances

Determine the animal's disposition in a hurry. Is it conscious of your presence in the room? Do you get the impression that it is curious, threatening, or aggressive? This evaluation will serve as the basis for your further actions.

Do not attempt to flee

Many different kinds of animals will become more aggressive if they are forced to run. Hold on to your position.

Create the Appearance That You Are Much Larger

Raise your arms, open your jacket, or hold something in front of you to make yourself appear larger and more menacing.

Make some racket!

Talk in a commanding manner with a strong, low voice. Do not yell, but make sure that your voice is audible enough to let others know you are there.

Stay away from their eyes

Eye contact that is unavoidable might be misinterpreted as an invitation to fight. Instead, make it your goal to always have the animal in the periphery of your view.

Create some space by moving slowly

You should start backing away from the animal without turning your back on it and preferably moving in the direction in which you came from.

Put on Your Protective Equipment

If the animal continues to approach you despite these precautions, you should use your bear spray or another type of safety gear and aim it towards the animal's face
.

Following the Occurrence

Once the animal has left the area, you should make a hasty but non-running retreat to a location that is more secure as soon as possible. Inform other hikers about the incident and report it to the appropriate authorities in the area.

Your actions will play a crucial part in determining the result of any encounters you have with creatures that are potentially dangerous to you. In precarious circumstances like this, your greatest lines of defense are information and preparedness. Keep in mind that the purpose of this is to ensure not only your safety but also the animal's safety. The vast majority of wild animals would rather not associate with people; thus, it is important to know how to diffuse potentially volatile situations so that everyone involved may escape unscathed.

Chapter 10

First Aid Basics

Recognizing and Treating Cuts and Scrapes

Exploring the great outdoors may be an exhilarating and freeing experience for people of any age; nevertheless, there is always the possibility of suffering from a small injury, such as a cut or scratch. Even the most seasoned campers are not immune to the usual injuries that may be sustained in the great outdoors. Some examples of these injuries include slipping and falling on a wet rock, getting scratched by a prickly shrub, or getting a cut with a pocket knife. To avoid infections and other consequences, it is essential to be able to detect the symptoms and administer the appropriate treatment for them.

The Different Kinds of Cuts and Scrapes

Minor surface lacerations and more severe gashes can both be caused by cuts and scrapes. Scratches that are only superficial affect only the outermost layer of the skin.
Cuts that are shallow involve just the top layer of the skin and maybe the very top of the underlying tissue.

Deep cuts are those that penetrate the skin and impact the tissues and perhaps the muscle beneath it.
Immediate Reaction: A Primer on First-Aid Essentials

Purge the Cut or Wound

The first and most important step is to thoroughly clean the wound using soap and water that is uncontaminated. In the event that you do not have access to soap, properly cleaning the wound with water can also assist in the removal of dirt and debris. Avoid using alcohol and hydrogen peroxide as much as possible since they both have the potential to cause tissue damage and slow the healing process.

Determine the Degree of Severity

Is it only a light scratch, or is there more of a cut there? Does it bleed a much when you cut it? The severity of the situation will dictate the following actions.

Utilize Some Force

When treating wounds that are bleeding, applying pressure with a clean cloth or gauze might enable the blood to clot. Raise the injured location higher above the level of the heart to stop the flow of blood.
Utilize an antiseptic
To reduce the likelihood of being infected, use an antiseptic ointment if you have access to one. On the other hand, it is not a replacement for thorough cleaning.

Take Care of the Cut

Wrap the wound in sterile gauze or a bandage to prevent it from becoming contaminated and to shield it from any more harm.

When to Seek the Assistance of a Qualified Medical Professional

The incision is rather deep, and the margins of the wound are quite apart from one another.
The wound has a foreign item that is implanted in it.
Even after applying pressure to the wound for a number of minutes, the bleeding does not cease.
Infection is indicated by the development of symptoms such as increased redness, swelling, or pus.

Upkeep in addition to Supervision

After the initial treatment, it is extremely important to continue to monitor the wound in order to look for any symptoms of infection. At the very least, you should replace the dressing every day, and you should do it more frequently if it gets soiled or moist. Maintain the regular use of the antibacterial ointment as directed.

Every young adventurer needs to be able to identify and properly treat minor wounds, such as cuts and scratches, when they occur. It gives you the ability to treat ordinary injuries with confidence and lowers the likelihood that small wounds may progress into more serious issues. Not only will you protect your health and well-being by putting together a simple first aid kit and educating yourself on how to administer simpler treatments, but you will also get more out of your time spent in the great outdoors. After all, an explorer who is pleased is an adventurer who is well-prepared.

What to Do in Case of Bites or Stings

Even with all of its charm and mystery, the natural world is home to a wide array of species that are capable of biting or stinging. Even while most interactions with wildlife are completely safe, you should always be prepared in case they bite or sting you. Anyone who spends time outside in the woods should be prepared for the possibility of being bitten or stung by any number of animals, ranging from ants and bees to snakes and spiders.

Different types of stings and bites

There are several potential causes of bites and stings, including the following:

• Bee, wasp, and hornet stings are examples of venomous insect bites.

• Bites from Spiders: Including Those Caused by the Brown Recluse and the Black Widow

• There are two types of snake bites: venomous and non-venomous.

• Bites from Mammals: Such as those received from a Raccoon or a Bat

• Aquatic Bites and Stings: These can come from marine organisms such as jellyfish or stingrays.

Immediate Intervention: First-Aid Procedures

Keep your cool

Your heart rate will only increase if you allow yourself to become panicked, which may hasten the spread of any venom or poisons that are in your circulation. Maintain as much composure as you can and encourage those around you to do the same.

Determine who is to blame

If you know what bit or stung you, you can more accurately identify what therapy will be most helpful. If it is feasible to do so, you should make a note of the creature's size, color, and any other distinctive characteristics.

Take Out the Stingers

In the case of bee stings, use an item with a flat edge to scrape the stinger out of the skin if it is still embedded there. Do not use tweezers since the act of squeezing might cause additional venom to be released.

Clean up the Area

Soap and cold water should be used to gently clean the wound. Scrubbing should be avoided since it may make the situation worse.

Use some ice

Applying something cool to the affected area might help decrease swelling and dull the discomfort. Ice should never be applied directly to the skin; instead, it should be wrapped in a towel or a plastic bag before being applied.

Raise the Level of the Area

Raise the afflicted limb or area of the body as much as you can to reduce the amount of edema.

Antihistamines and pain relievers should be taken.

Antihistamines that are available without a prescription, such as Benadryl, can help reduce the stinging and swelling that result from bug bites or stings. Only use in the manner specified.

When to Seek the Assistance of a Qualified Medical Professional

having trouble breathing, swelling of the face or lips, or a severe rash are some of the signs of an allergic response.

The perpetrator is a toxic animal, such a snake with venom, for example.

Symptoms indicate an infection, such as red streaks, pus, or an increase in both pain and swelling.

After being bitten by an animal, you are concerned about whether or not you are protected against tetanus.

Monitoring Following an Incident

For the next few days, keep an eye on the region where you were bitten or stung for any indications of infection or an allergic response. Even if the symptoms aren't too severe right away, issues may still arise in the future.

Being prepared for bites and stings is an essential component of safe behavior in the outdoors, despite the fact that no one wants to think about the unpleasant possibilities. A basic first aid pack that contains necessities such as antiseptics and antihistamines may go a long way toward treating an injury or illness. Not only may recognizing the symptoms and being aware of how to respond in a timely manner reduce suffering, but it can also save lives. You will be able to appreciate your trips into the outdoors with a better sense of calm if you are knowledgeable and well-prepared.

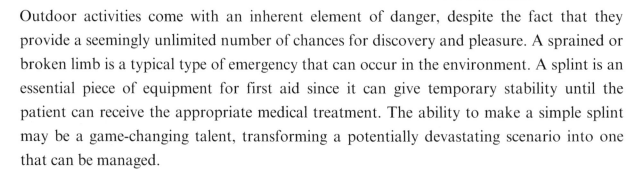

Outdoor activities come with an inherent element of danger, despite the fact that they provide a seemingly unlimited number of chances for discovery and pleasure. A sprained or broken limb is a typical type of emergency that can occur in the environment. A splint is an essential piece of equipment for first aid since it can give temporary stability until the patient can receive the appropriate medical treatment. The ability to make a simple splint may be a game-changing talent, transforming a potentially devastating scenario into one that can be managed.

The Elements That Make Up a Splint

The primary purpose of a splint is to immobilize a limb that has been fractured or sprained so as to prevent the limb from being further injured. Pain relief, reduction in swelling, and protection against further injury to muscles, nerves, and blood vessels are just some of the benefits that may be gained by properly constructing a splint.

Materials That You May Make Use Of

The great outdoors provides a wealth of raw materials that may be fashioned into simple splints, including the following:

• Rigid Objects such as sticks, hiking poles, or even a newspaper that has been wrapped up
.

• Bandanas, shoelaces, belts, or pieces of fabric can be used as ties.

• Clothing, leaves, or moss can be used as padding.

• A Basic Splint: A Guide with Detailed Step-by-Step Instructions

Consider the Circumstances

Conduct a thorough assessment to establish whether or not a splint is required for the injury. Examine the area carefully for any indications of shattered bones, such as deformity, edema, and excruciating pain.

Adjust the Angle of the Limb

Before putting the splint, the limb should be repositioned into a position that is as close to its natural and comfortable state as feasible. Do not attempt to straighten shattered bones on your own; instead, get medical attention for the issue.

Make ready the material that is rigid

Locate or get ready the piece of hard material that will act as the splint. Make sure it is long enough to immobilize the joint both above and below where the damage is located.

Put Down Some Padding

When the hard material comes into touch with the damaged region, use padding to reduce the amount of additional discomfort that it causes. Make use of clothes, leaves, or anything else soft that you have on hand.

Put the splint together

Make use of whatever knots you have available (a bandana, your shoelaces, etc.) in order to fasten the hard material to the limb. Be sure that it is snug enough to keep the splint in place without being so tight that it prevents blood from flowing through the area.

Examine the flow of blood

After the splint has been properly fastened, it is extremely important to check that the patient's blood circulation has not been impaired. Check to see whether there is a pulse underneath the splint, and keep an eye out for any indications of tingling, numbness, or the skin becoming blue.

When to Seek the Assistance of a Qualified Medical Professional

A splint that you make yourself is only a stopgap solution. As quickly as possible, seek the examination and treatment of a trained medical practitioner, particularly in the event that there is an open fracture, significant pain, or evidence of infection.

When it comes to having fun in nature, one of the most useful skills you may have is the ability to build a simple splint. Accidents may happen at the most inopportune times, and being out in the woods removes the safety net of having fast access to expert medical treatment. If you have a basic understanding of first aid and how to apply splints, you will be able to respond efficiently in the event of an emergency, which will make your time spent in the wilderness both safer and more fulfilling.

Chapter 11

Useful Wilderness Crafts

Making Simple Tools
and
Utensils from Nature

The sensation of being outdoors and at one with nature is energizing and rewarding; yet, what do you do if you discover that you are missing some vital equipment or utensils? Whether it's the discovery that you've forgotten your camping spoon or the regrettable loss of a crucial instrument, nature will frequently give what you need; all you have to do is learn how to use it. In this manual, we will discuss how to make straightforward instruments and utensils out of natural materials, so combining ingenuity with a reverence for the natural world.

The First and Most Important Rule: Make Do With What You Have

Utilizing what is immediately accessible is an essential component of any survival strategy. To our good fortune, mother nature provides a plethora of resources. The natural environment contains a wide variety of possible tools, ranging from twigs to stones, leaves to vines, and everything in between.

Instruments for Cutting

1. A Knife Made of Stone

Find a stone with a granular consistency, such as chert or flint, and use that. It is possible to make sharp flakes that can be utilized as cutting tools by hitting the edge of the rock with another hard rock. These are ideal for cutting through cordage and may even be used to chop meat if you are in a panic.

2. A knife made of bamboo

You are in luck if you happen to be in an area that has bamboo. A piece of broken bamboo can be used as the blade of a very sharp knife.

Equipment for Digging

1. Trowel on a Stick

When digging, a stick that is strong and flat can serve as an excellent shovel. Choose a piece of wood that has a width that's adequate for moving dirt but is yet manageable for comfortable holding. The finer the timber, the more robust it should be.

2. A scoop made of bone or shell

Additionally, bones from animals or huge shells can function as digging equipment. Because of the inherent curve of their edges, they are ideally suited for scooping dirt.

Kitchenware and tableware

1. A Spoon or Spork Made of Wood

Find a branch that has a little stubby offshoot on one end; this will function as the handle. Make a bowl for the spoon by carving it out with a knife (or a stone flake, if you like). If necessary, sand it down with a stone that is smoother.

2. a pair of chopsticks

Get a hold of a couple of straight twigs. Cut back any side branches and make them as even as possible. You now have some improvised chopsticks in your possession.

Equipment for Fishing and Hunting

1. Fishing Hachette

A simple fish hook can be fashioned from a piece of bone or a thorn, depending on the material available. As a fishing line, you may make it by attaching it to a vine or a thin strip of bark.

2. Rappelling device

The base of a slingshot can be made out of a strong branch in the shape of a Y. For the sling, you can make use of a piece of animal skin or sturdy plant fibers.

3. Captures of Animals

Sticks, pebbles, and vines may all be used to create basic animal traps like snares and pitfall traps using the materials at hand.

Packing materials

Packing materials

1. Cup Made of Leaves

Simple cups or bowls may be made by folding and pinning together large, strong leaves such as banana leaves.

2. Container made of Bamboo

A piece of bamboo can be used as a container for transporting liquids or keeping food, such as water. Put a layer of dirt or soft leaves at the bottom to seal it.

Equipment for Starting a Fire

1. An archery drill

You'll need a sturdy stick with a curved end for the bow, a piece of wood with a flat surface for the fireboard, a smaller stick for the spindle, and some cordage or a strip of clothing for the string in order to complete this project.

2. An open flame plough

The base can be made out of a piece of wood that is softer, while the plough can be made out of a stick that is tougher and pointed. The tinder may be ignited by creating heat with the plough by rubbing it around the base.

The Values Associated with Being Resourceful

When developing these tools, it is essential to keep in mind the effect that they will have on the surrounding ecosystem. Take only what you need, and make an effort to make use of resources that have died or fallen rather than harvesting from plants that are still alive. Being resourceful is not just a necessary survival ability; it is also an art form that combines creative expression with logical thinking. Your ability to fashion basic implements and implements from natural materials may not only make your time spent outdoors safer, but it can also make your time spent outside more fulfilling. Through establishing such a basic connection with the natural world, you open the door to a more in-depth awareness of the environment around you as well as your capabilities to traverse it. This is a skill set that, regardless of whether you are a newbie outdoorsperson or an experienced adventurer, will make your time spent in the woods more enjoyable in more ways than one.

Conclusion

As we come to the end of this Wilderness Survival Guide for Kids, it is crucial to understand that the lessons you've learned go beyond simply surviving in the woods. Instead, they welcome you into a relationship with the natural world that will last for the rest of your life. The path that you embark on each time you go into the wilderness is not only about prevailing over nature; rather, it is about learning to live in harmony with it in a way that is sustainable and respectful. Every plant that you name, every shelter that you construct, and every route that you travel is a conversation with the land, and just like any other important discussion, it should be carried on with deliberation and respect.

A principle that is more fundamental than the need to survive is respect for nature. Realizing that you are only one component of a much broader ecosystem requires a commitment that will last a lifetime. When you are learning how to make tools from natural materials, it is important to keep in mind that each resource plays an important part in the natural ecosystem in which it was found. Therefore, just use what you require, and give items that have fallen or died more priority than living plants and trees from which to harvest. You must ensure that you do not leave any traces behind, whether it is trash, harm, or even the residue of your activity. The preservation of the natural habitat not only helps to keep the ecosystem's delicate balance intact, but it also assures that future explorers will be able to experience the same spectacular splendor that you have.

As you go on your journeys, remember to keep this ethic of care and respect with you at all times. Make it as essential to your outdoor activities as your bag and the footwear you wear hiking and camping. Keep in mind, though, that despite their name, adventures are supposed to be risk-free. Consequently, as you prepare, you shouldn't simply think about what foods to carry or what routes to climb; you should also think about how to deal with any potential dangers that you could encounter. Always let someone know where you plan to go and what time you anticipate getting back. Continue to hone your survival abilities not just so that you may take on more difficult adventures, but also so that you can reduce the hazards that are involved with such activities.

The more experience and expertise you have, the less risk you are going to be exposed to on your travels. This does not mean that you should completely avoid taking any chances; after all, getting out of your comfort zone is frequently where the real fun and excitement is. To achieve success, you must, nevertheless, learn to take measured risks that you are ready to manage. To this purpose, you should never cease expanding your knowledge. Continue learning new things, getting better at what you already know, and most importantly, never stop exploring the great outdoors. Your travels will take you on a path to become a more responsible, skillful, and enlightened individual; they will not just be a voyage through the woods.

So, here's to many more excursions that are both safe and rewarding in the years to come. I wish that your adoration for nature would always be accompanied with a healthy dose of reverence for it, and that each excursion would not only deepen your knowledge of the world around you but also help you better appreciate your place in it.

Made in United States
Troutdale, OR
10/30/2023

14167377R00060